FORTUNA

T0009508

"With his customary scholarly zeal, Nigel Pennick's nevertheless accessible examination of our love/hate relationship with fortune, or luck, throughout history takes us deeply into the interlocked worlds of religion and superstition—with a fair sprinkling of human foolishness. With diverse quotations from the likes of the Oracle of Delphi and George Orwell's *1984* and locations from ancient Egypt to the gambling dens of the Deep South, this uniquely thorough history of luck is comprehensive, riveting, and intriguing."

LYNN PICKNETT AND CLIVE PRINCE,
AUTHORS OF *WHEN GOD HAD A WIFE*

"From the ancient Roman oracle of Praeneste to the geomantic potato divination of Essex, from Dame Fortuna to Lady Luck, Nigel Pennick explores the guiding principle of both gambling and divination. He spreads a table of delights where number, probability, and randomness each turn Fortuna's Wheel."

CAITLÍN AND JOHN MATTHEWS,
AUTHORS OF *THE LOST BOOK OF THE GRAIL*

"Can fate and fortune be foretold or even changed? In this extraordinary new book, Nigel Pennick considers what fortune really is and how, over the years, people have sought to control it. He examines how it has fascinated artists, scientists, and philosophers and explores the many fascinating forms of divination and prediction employed over time. Wonderfully written, *Fortuna: The Sacred and Profane Faces of Luck* is a must for anyone who wonders what the future may hold."

GRAHAM PHILLIPS, AUTHOR OF *THE MYSTERY OF DOGGERLAND*

"With a scholar's rigorous research and a sage's wisdom, Pennick has crafted this multifaceted picture of Lady Luck, ranging from the history of oracles, divination, and games of chance to the many marvelous ways people have courted fortune's favor through the ages—including badger's teeth sewn into a pocket and special incense that burns away to reveal lucky numbers—and much, much more. *Fortuna* is a work of fascinating and thought-provoking beauty."

CAIT JOHNSON, AUTHOR OF
WITCH WISDOM FOR MAGICAL AGING

"In *Fortuna,* established wisdomkeeper Nigel Pennick delves into the many faces of predicting fortune, writing yet another authentic and engrossing book. I find it impossible to read without pausing every page to say to anyone in the room, 'Did you know . . . ?' Another definitive and fascinating work; highly recommended."

JUNE KENT, PUBLISHER OF *INDIE SHAMAN* MAGAZINE

"Pennick begins with a near-poetic overview of the human condition as stuck in a merciless complexity of variables on a celestial omnibus with a one-way driver: time. With his characteristic clarity of observation and attention to detail, he serves as a brilliant tour guide through the infinite continuum of attempts to quell the anxiety of the murky uncertainty of the journey. Persistent among these seek the intercession of goddess Fortuna/Lady Luck, their minions and practitioners, purporting to speak through the language of the universe—numbers. This is an entertaining and thoughtful book— and even offers several DIY prognostication techniques used over time to (possibly) help readers' navigate life decisions."

LINDA KELSEY-JONES, PRESIDENT OF THE
SAN MARCOS AREA ARTS COUNCIL AND DIRECTOR/CURATOR
OF THE WALKERS' GALLERY, SAN MARCOS

"With his customary insight, Nigel Pennick investigates the underlying principles and rationale of divination, the means by which the diviner may appeal to the gods (or the subconscious) for guidance, in order to change the course of their luck. Nigel examines methods from bones to dice, to oracle books and geomancy, including an old method of using the eyes on potatoes to foretell the future!"

ANNA FRANKLIN, AUTHOR OF *THE HEARTH WITCH'S COMPENDIUM*

FORTUNA

The Sacred and Profane
Faces of Luck

NIGEL PENNICK

Destiny Books
Rochester, Vermont

Destiny Books
One Park Street
Rochester, Vermont 05767
www.DestinyBooks.com

Text stock is SFI certified

Destiny Books is a division of Inner Traditions International

Copyright © 2024 by Nigel Pennick

All rights reserved. No part of this book may be reproduced or utilized in any form
or by any means, electronic or mechanical, including photocopying, recording, or by
any information storage and retrieval system, without permission in writing from the
publisher.

Cataloging-in-Publication Data for this title is available from the Library of Congress

ISBN 978-1-64411-647-0 (print)
ISBN 978-1-64411-648-7 (ebook)

Printed and bound in the United States by Lake Book Manufacturing, LLC
The text stock is SFI certified. The Sustainable Forestry Initiative® program promotes
sustainable forest management.

10   9   8   7   6   5   4   3   2   1

Text design and layout by Virginia Scott Bowman
This book was typeset in Garamond Premier Pro and Gill Sans with Ribelano and
Optima used as display typefaces

To send correspondence to the author of this book, mail a first-class letter to the
author c/o Inner Traditions • Bear & Company, One Park Street, Rochester, VT
05767, and we will forward the communication.

Tempora labuntur, tacitisque senescimus annis; et fugiunt fraeno non remorante dies.

The times speed onward, and we grow old as the years pass unnoticed; and the days pass with no brake to hold them back.

TYCHE. FORTUNA.

CONTENTS

Fig. I.1 Wheel of Fortune from Nigel Pennick's Tarot, 1990.

INTRODUCTION

The ancients, struck with this irreducibleness of the elements of human life to calculation, exalted chance into a divinity.

RALPH WALDO EMERSON

ate and destiny—matters of life and death—are of paramount importance to all humans. "What will become of me?" is a question that everyone must ask at some time. We cannot know the future, for the future is that which has not happened yet. Certain future events are known, such as the inevitability of aging, should we live so long, and death. But the duration of life and the events that may occur, whether beneficial or detrimental, are unknown. Ancient peoples understood that humans are subject to higher powers; the cycle of day and night, the seasons, weather, and natural disasters. These higher powers were ascribed to the actions of divine beings who caused these events by acts of their will. Certain disasters were presaged by natural signs, such as a strong wind bringing destructive rainfall that destroyed crops.

These were seen as warnings from the divine beings that something bad was to happen. So the idea emerged that it was possible to foretell certain events of a different order. Clearly, the divine powers were all-powerful when they decided to produce a disaster, so they must also predetermine the fates of human beings. These powers were personified as gods, and in ancient Greece the goddess Tyche and, for the Romans, Fortuna presided over the fortunes of people. Her edicts, it was believed, determined in advance the good luck or otherwise of individuals, and their ultimate fate.

People who predicted, whether by chance or intuition, events that later took place, were considered mouthpieces of the divine powers able to deliver oracular answers to those who questioned them about their future. The oracular pronouncements of successful seers were collected together and became texts that, when organized in a systematic order with numbers, could be consulted. Because in the ancient worldview nothing happens by chance but is the manifestation of an act of divine will, casting certain objects that produce a number, such as cowrie shells or dice of various kinds, provided access to one or other of these oracular systems. The number produced by what we in modern times call random was seen as directly willed by the deity invoked in the ritual of casting cowries or dice. Many profane human pastimes and sports began as sacred rites to contact or honor divine powers. Wine drinking was an integral part of the rites of the god Dionysus and later a sacrament of Christianity; tobacco smoking began as a sacred ritual of the Indigenous peoples of the Americas; surfing was a religious act performed in the inauguration ceremonies of the kings of Hawaii when it was an independent nation; and the use of dice harks back to a time when homage was paid to Fortuna before they became a means of gambling.

A tradition among Icelandic gamblers holds that Odin, the one-eyed god of consciousness and insight, was the inventor of dice. The tumbling dice, though random and only predictable in the long run through the principles of statistical probability, produce a real and immediate outcome. When the dice are rolled, a state of temporary liminality is brought into being. As they roll, the outcome is imminent, yet it is not yet determined. Once the dice come to rest, the outcome is present and cannot be altered. The random immediately becomes determinate the moment the dice roll to a halt. Whatever the result, it has a stark and immediate presence, and when given human significance, the points on the twelve faces of the pair of dice can bring fortune or ruin. When the dice are at rest, the success or failure of our predicament is at once apparent. Such is the nature of gambling and a metaphor for the nature of life.

Using dice and similar devices for divination is the spiritual side of this moment of liminality, a random means of enabling us to consider life questions that do not lend themselves to linear thought. Divination enables us to transfer decision-making from the realm of the rational and the emotional into another, nonnormal level of cognition. The state of being we call reality is perplexingly multidimensional, and so, whatever technique we may use to gain extrasensory knowledge—cards, dice, divinatory geomancy, oracle books, and so on—will give us new, unthought-of, unexpected insights into the situation. Although divination has a seemingly random operating system, the outcome is eminently practical for it provides the means to think about and understand problems in another way. This is the unique value and promise of divination.

NIGEL CAMPBELL PENNICK
OLD ENGLAND HOUSE

THE MYTHS OF TIME

....

*The Impossibility of Originality
in the Universal Laws*

here is a strong wish by anyone who studies the cultures of the past to take the fragments we possess and attempt to piece them together to make a whole. In some measure, this can be done with a pot or bottle found in an archaeological dig, so long as all the pieces remain, but it is not possible with something as intangible as human culture. Unfortunately, in many quarters there is an unquestioned assumption that for any aspect of past culture there was a coherent whole, like a pot, which although currently broken into many fragments can be pieced together again to restore an integrated structure that is the same as the "original." This assumption falls apart when we apply to it the question: What was the whole that we are attempting to reconstruct? There is no cultural whole of anything we may choose to examine that existed at any one time. If we look at the present, can we define the whole of any part of culture that may appear to be a category or unit? What is the whole of Great Britain or the United States at the moment you read this? The whole of science? The whole of art? Impossible to answer because the question, and the nature of the data required, is indeterminate in meaning.

The words we use, such as *whole,* give the illusion that they are the reality they name. But language is only a metaphor we use to exist in the world as conscious beings and to attempt to communicate with other people about everything we need to do to live. Words like *whole, restore, dog,* and *god* are not objective truths but sounds uttered by humans who speak English to signify particular parts of existence that we (along with Aristotle) deem to be discrete "objects," somehow separate from everything else that surrounds them and of which they are part.

The arbitrary nature of these words is obvious for there are many other languages using totally different words to signify the same objects we have names for in English. For English itself as I write it now is the result of continuous change, making it unintelligible to a speaker of Anglo-Saxon Old English twelve hundred years ago could they be brought forward in time to read it. This in itself demonstrates the mutable, metaphorical nature of language, and the questionable special pleading of those who claim certain ancient languages as they were spoken at a particular time in history, are "holy."

The belief that there can be, or *should* be, unequivocal and transparent forms of reality, manifested as correct culture, is clearly false. But the belief that there is *one and only one* correct interpretation, and all else is error, is the principle of the infallibility of the pope of Rome and many other belief systems that came before and after that office was invented. Religions that have a written liturgy, or equally a fully scored opera, may appear to have a coherence that defines every parameter of how they should be performed. But because they are expressed in language, these laws, prescriptions, scores, and diktats are inevitably incomplete, and it is necessary for someone to interpret them for their desires to be made real in the physical world. Hence priests, theologians, investigative panels, interpreters, conductors, lawyers, courts, judges, and other ritual specialists have existed as long as there have been written codes to interpret.

Injustice, persecutions, sectarianism, and wars have emerged and do emerge from variant interpretations of the same text. And the nature of each subsequent performance of such scripted and even unscripted cultural events means that it must be different from the previous one. André Malraux called this phenomenon "the persisting life of certain forms reemerging again and again like specters from the past" (Malraux 1978, 13). Nothing can be identical to anything else, even if it is an exact replica, for it is a second example of whatever is being reproduced. Even each rerun of a mechanical or electronic recording takes place at a different time and in a different context from the time and place it was recorded. Although commerce and the heritage industry behave as though reconstruction is possible, contemporary art has broken free from that assumption. For example, John Cage observed that if we think that things are being repeated it is generally because we are not paying attention to all of the details. But if we pay attention as if we were looking through a microscope at all the details, we can see that there is no such thing as repetition (Cage, 1997).

The broken pot that is pieced together by the archaeological reconstructors and appears to be whole again is in its present condition because of an action different from that which made it originally. In fact, it is not actually whole, for it has been reassembled by adhesives that hold the broken parts together. It lost its coherence when it was smashed, and that state can never be recovered. The object has a history, even if it is irrevocably lost and cannot

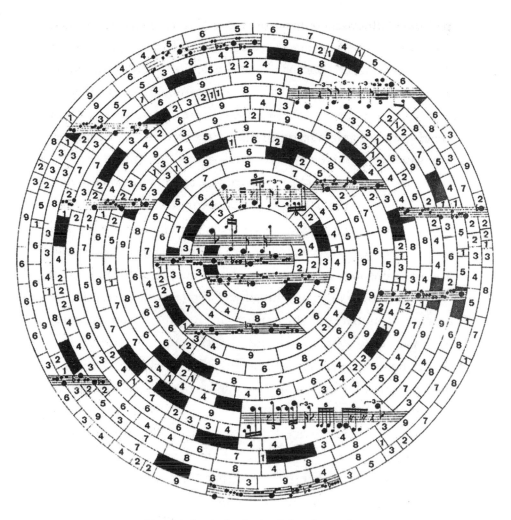

Fig. 1.1 Score by León Calancha under
the tutelage of John Cage in Tangier, 2014.
(Courtesy of Cineutopia)

be retold. The incidents that resulted in the pot being broken and
buried and the incidents of it being dug up and pieced together
are all part of its history. In the museum, however, the pot is presented as an object without any of this history; it becomes a historical object, which, if famous, is called an "iconic piece."

Because, despite the above, many believe that the past can be reconstructed, and a credible narrative about the past called "history" can be constructed where cause and effect is shown to have been in action, the concept of the future was invented. Because the past was once the future, and in it cause and effect can be demonstrated as having "led" from one state to the next, emerged the idea that the future is also reconstructible in advance and che serà, serà—what will be, will be—and in a predetermined way.

Predestination is an important doctrine within religions whose operative theory states that there is an all-powerful god that has planned the existence of the world in advance, and consequently the present is just the place we are at in the finished cosmic video currently being played. Clearly, this is a belief that does not admit to anything happening outside the script; it renders all human life and actions meaningless. Even attempts to predict the future are already programmed into the actions that happen; all human acts of love and cruelty, benevolence or destruction are inevitable enactments of the perverse cosmic puppet master's game.

It is clear that this total determinism in advance was not a belief of most religious teachings of the past. Free will, which means life existing in real time rather than as a replay of the Creator's finished script, means that by our actions we can change the present and affect what happens in the future. Having knowledge, we may make decisions that produce a good outcome, and divination may give answers to dilemmas that we may encounter. Oracles operate on this principle: they may give wise answers to questions that are posited, or they may indicate the inevitability of a particular outcome. If one is told that one will die if one takes a particular planned journey, and then one decides not to go and is still alive after the time the journey would have been taken, then the dire possibility has been averted. It is impossible to tell what would have happened if . . .

VERIFIABLE PHENOMENA AND THE "LAWS" OF NATURE

If a phenomenon can be verified by some means external to the phenomenon, it is said to exist, and that is the criterion of validity in both science and law. But from this "fact" of verifiability comes a fallacy that overrides the limits of its usefulness and describes all of reality in the same way, for it does not mean that if a phenomenon is not verifiable it does *not* exist. But most of thinking and human understanding of the nature of existence revolves around a belief in this fallacy. Although it is common to the point of being an unconscious assumption, it is of the same order as the fallacy that because all dogs are animals, all animals are dogs. This is clearly wrong, and so is the belief that absence of evidence is evidence of absence, or even that absence of evidence is meaningful at all. Verifiable phenomena are the basis of science and technology, and the predictable behavior of some events and objects gave rise a long time ago to the idea that these happenings are indicative of the "laws" of nature.

The word *law* infers that there is a human law giver, which originates implicitly from early civilization when winning warlords called themselves kings and issued edicts that others were forced to obey, for those who did not obey were tortured and killed. In order to validate their laws, these ancient hard men frequently claimed that their power was part of a divine order. Their edicts, this theory claimed, were issued by the gods or God, depending on whether they had a polytheistic or a monotheistic interpretation of divinity. If one believes that laws come directly from the divine source, then it is impossible to question, develop, or change them, and they must remain fixed from the moment of their invention. Hence the monarch of the United Kingdom of Great Britain and Northern Ireland in the twenty-first century claims to be there *Dei gratia* (by the grace of God) and is head of the Church of England and boasts the socially divisive title *Fidei Defensor,* Defender of the Faith. Human power always claims supernatural backing, for then awkward questions about legitimacy can be legally labeled blasphemous and the critics punished accordingly without the relevant questions ever having to be answered.

Many religions view the Creator in the form of an angry Bronze Age law-making warlord who decides how the natural world must behave and who issues the laws that define those behaviors. These so-called laws of nature are viewed as fixed in the same way as the religious laws claimed to originate in some particular godhead. Early science, which developed from religious sources, also believed in ultimate laws of nature, ever seeking to elucidate them. Observers over thousands of years have looked at how the world works and found that in some (limited) cases what happens can be explained as cause and effect, or the supposed principle of the law of causation. *Cause and effect* is a phrase used by humans to describe a certain part of the reality we experience; it is not an external principle operating outside of what actually happens. Because certain objects behave in a particular predictable way, it is assumed that they are "obeying" ultimate laws like a subservient human subject of the ancient warlord's territory. This observation and predictability cannot be extended to the belief that there are ultimate laws—or even "mechanisms," to use an alternative industrial metaphor—being obeyed. But this does not stop people from doing it and setting up whole philosophical systems around the belief. They forget that neither the legalistic worldview of the laws of nature nor the engineering view of mechanisms is reality. They are at best only human attempts to invent a workable relational and descriptive theory of existence.

The concepts of randomness and mathematical probability are absent in ancient writings that ascribe all events to the agency of divine beings. Mathematics had not then reached the stage where probability could be thought of and evaluated. Religions that claim the existence of an all-knowing, all-powerful God teach that every event that takes place is under the direct control of God. Nothing can happen without God's agency. God's will controls everything down to the last drop of rain, and a consequence of this theory is that everything that happens is preordained; all events have been decided in advance by God and are unchangeable. Period.

Randomness is a concept outside this deterministic belief system. Often the word *random* is used to denote unpredictable, incoherent, haphazard, or chaotic happenings; actions done without conscious choice or method, having no purpose or objective. Randomness is described formally in mathematics and statistics. Mathematically, the concept of randomness is not chaotic, but it signifies a lack of predictability, which nevertheless is bounded by laws of probability. It is this kind of randomness that is important in divination systems that use numbers to denote readings. Assigning a numerical value to each possible outcome of an event produces what is known as a random variable. This allows the probabilities of the events to be calculated. A sequence of random variables that describe a process with nondeterministic outcomes but which follow a process ruled by probability is called a random process.

Science, law, divination, magic, and religion are not reality; they are methods for investigating reality. Often, they embed within their methods archaic linguistic concepts, ways of thinking about the world that have been disproved, such as the geocentric universe. All of these human constructs actually work in the limited areas from which they come, but their deterministic theories fail when they claim to be applicable to everything in all of space and time.

The discovery of the laws of probability provided a means of describing what percentage of occurrences of an event is likely to take place over the long run; it tells us nothing about what the outcome of the next occurrence will be. There appears to be determinism over the long run. For instance, when a die is thrown thousands of times, the percentage of results likely will more and more approximate the mathematical probability. But that does not mean that ten throws of a die will not produce ten sixes in a row.

From the long-term mathematical probability has emerged the myth of the maturity of chances, which says that a result is more likely if it has not turned up in a while. Cricket enthusiasts may remember England captain Nasser Hussain, who lost fourteen test match coin tosses in a row. He was considered unlucky, but the fifteenth toss, had it happened, still had a fifty-fifty chance of heads or tails coming up, as had the fourteen he lost. It was irrelevant that he had lost fourteen; even if the same coin were used, it has no memory.

TOSSING HEADS OR TAILS

John Ashton notes that in ancient Greece and Rome, "they also tossed 'head or tail,' betting on which side a piece of money, thrown up in the air, would come down. The Greeks used for this game a shell, black on one side, white on the other, and called it 'night or day.' The Romans used a copper *as* with the head of Janus on one side, and the prow of a galley on the other, and they called their game *Capita aut navim* (head or ship)" (Ashton 1898, 10). A coin or a disc with different colors on each face is used to decide by the team captains in football (soccer) and cricket as to the direction of play or who should bat first.

WORDS, MEANING, AND FALSEHOOD

In her kitchen, the police recovered knives that could be used as murder weapons.

The oracles of antiquity were famed for their accuracy, yet many of the pronouncements we know of were actually imprecise and ambiguous. Their very ambiguity could often describe any possible outcome, and afterward were seen as predictive of what actually occurred (as with the oracles of Napoleon presented below). Present-day politicians, officials, businessmen, soldiers, and lawyers have a comparable form of language that is at once intricate and empty. Their statements are couched in complex assemblages of words that, when heard, sound as though they are full of meaning, but when they are analyzed they are exposed as tautological, repetitive mixed metaphors. The "sea changes" and "tip of the icebergs" are interspersed with more extended, formal excursions into attenuated hyperbole. We've all heard political business speak like "The only option that limits our options is the option that gives us no options," meaningless phrases like "a poorly performing rate of improvement," or complex repetitive explanations like "What we are doing is using resources more sensibly for the future. The future use of resources sensibly used will enable us to outsource future resources more sensibly, resourcing their use to enable the future resources sensibly to be outsourced at the end of the day." Because they are imprecise, and appear in predictive language, like ancient oracles, they can be interpreted in many ways by different listeners and cannot be proven wrong.

In the early twentieth century, such ways of speaking would have been presented as avant-garde poetry by practitioners of Futurism or Dada at artists' cabarets in Milan or Zürich. We are so used to hearing men in suits making such statements today that they pass without comment. So we can switch on the radio and hear, masquerading as news, statements like "The president announced that four hundred militants have been killed in the present attempt to cut down on violence" as the BBC Radio 4 news told us without a hint of irony at 4:00 p.m. on February 24, 2007. Political and business speak is a version of the "newspeak" predicted by George Orwell in his dystopian 1948 novel, *1984,* where the use of language has been so degraded that words cease to convey their meaning.

Around the same time, the Irish writer Myles na gCopaleen, who wrote under a number of names including Flann O'Brien (his anglicized official name was Brian O'Nolan, the Irish of which was Brian O'Nuaillain, and he is believed to have written under other names as well), created a series of newspaper articles titled *The Myles na gCopaleen Catechism of Cliché,* which pitilessly exposed the ritualized emptiness of such language (O'Brien 1993, 201–27).

But despite the best attempts of great writers to deconstruct the futility and expose the dangers of using of such persiflage, it always feels good when the experts tell us that we are on track to deliver integrated procurement, for this is quite a unique situation we find ourselves in at this moment in time. It is quite clear from all this that politicians' and business people's script writers are always striving not to tell the truth but to find the best way to be noncommittal "at the end of the day." Now we can stop worrying, for the government is in full control, there is light at the end of the tunnel, and we are all in this together. The spiritual oracles of old have been replaced in the collective sense by political and business speak that appears as a verbal and intellectual smokescreen. The whole paraphernalia of humbug and pretense serves to blur and mask the nefarious real intentions and actions of corporations and governments. Keep calm and carry on.

Traditionally in antiquity, oracles were present at special sacred places, of which Delphi in Greece is the most famous. There were two categories of oracle. In some places, a professional seeress or priestess would go into a trance, supposedly possessed by a divine power, and then was asked a question, which she would answer in the voice of the god. Replies were often ambiguous, as those who questioned were sometime powerful men, such as kings, who wished to know the outcome of their actions, such as whether to wage war. Replying directly in such cases was dangerous if the querent did not like the answer, and so as not to rouse the anger of an irascible warlord an ambiguous response was the most prudent course. "A great king will fall in battle" could be the answer to a monarch's question about his forthcoming war, and the proud king would assume it was his enemy who would die. When the battle took place, however, it was just as likely that he would die. The oracle was right either way. This sort of oracle, being human, could be positive—a means of warning powerful people against dangerous courses of action—but also it was open to fraud and manipulation.

The other sort of oracle at ancient shrines was impersonal, involving divination by means of marked items. Dice could produce numbers that referred to particular prophetic texts, or words could be written on sticks, chosen at random by an illiterate acolyte. This category of oracle had minimal human intervention but was still considered divine because they took place at a holy shrine and sacred rituals were performed before and during the divination that invoked the assistance of divine powers. Although in its functioning it was freed from the bias that spoken oracles may have had, the texts or words selected had already been written, which may have emphasized or omitted certain possible readings. Inevitably, all divination systems have built-in biases and gaps that stem from the abilities or interests of their originators. But in either case, the oracle given was deemed to come from the god or goddess to whom the shrine was dedicated and so was assumed to be a true prophecy.

LADY LUCK AND
THE GODDESS FORTUNA

....

Oracle of Numbers

If it wasn't for bad luck,
I wouldn't have no luck at all.

TRADITIONAL BLUES LYRIC

THE GODDESS FORTUNA, LADY LUCK,
AND THE PRAENESTINE ORACLE

Chance is defined as the way in which events happen and things fall out or a happening or occurrence of things in a particular way, perceived as a casual or fortuitous circumstance without conscious manipulation or a deterministic end. The outcome of chance is fortune—not in the sense of wealth that it often means but as the circumstances than ensue as the result of chance. Fortuna, the goddess of chance, luck, and fortune, is the personification of this

way that things happen or turn out. Chance also has an impersonal aspect: blind chance that can turn out well or ill for an individual. It is related to luck in that if by chance things turn out
well for an individual, that individual can be said to be lucky, but
if things turn out badly, that person is said to be unlucky. Luck
is viewed as a possession that has a certain capacity or amount.
When by chance things that have been going well suddenly change
for the worse and stop being favorable, we say that our luck has
run out. Whatever luck we had has been used up, and now it
no longer operates. If luck is seen as a series of fortunate coincidences (for us), then the coincidences have stopped happening.
Those who attempt to augment or extend their supply of luck call
upon Fortuna to smile upon them and bestow some more luck or
resume the sequence of fortunate coincidences, or *acausal ordered-
ness* as Carl Jung called it.

The goddess Fortuna presides over what would now be called
random events, chance, and luck. In the Roman Empire during
pagan times, Fortuna was the goddess of fate and fortune and naturally was sought out by those who wished to possess good luck
and foretell the future. While Fortuna is sometimes depicted with
wings, which connects her with the earlier Etruscan goddess of
fate, Nortia, she is conventionally depicted holding in one hand
a cornucopia, signifying that all good things come in abundance
from fortune. Indeed the cornucopia-wielding goddess Abundantia
may be seen as an aspect of Fortuna.

In Fortuna's other hand is a ship's rudder, denoting her
influence on how individuals' fates are steered. Her most famous
attribute is the vertically turning wheel of fortune, shown as part
of her throne. It is also one of the tarot trumps. This is the most
significant element of Fortuna's iconography, signifying the rise
and fall of all things. Inexorable in its progress, it favors none
above any other, for the wheel is an early historic recognition of

the principle of probability and the statistical outcome of random events. The wheel most simply denotes to us the ups and downs of life.

Fig. 2.1. Goddess Fortuna from
Andrew Tooke's The Fabulous Pantheon, 1764.
(Nigel Pennick Collection)

In Roman Italy, the goddess Fortuna was consulted in oracular shrines at Praeneste and Antium. The major shrine of Fortuna at Praeneste, now called Palestrina, had a magnificent temple that stood on top of a terraced holy mountain upon which were built the usual ancillary buildings and chapels for the clergy and

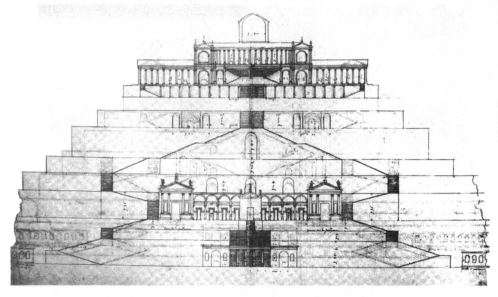

Fig. 2.2. Architect's sketch of Andrea Palladio's
Temple of Fortuna Primigenia reconstruction at Palestrina.
(Courtesy of the Royal Institute of British Architects,
London, Inv. IX/5)

pilgrims. The oracle of Fortuna was probably located in the complex of natural and excavated caves at the foot of the holy mountain where the Christians built a cathedral and seminary after they desecrated, looted, and destroyed the temples and appropriated the site. In the cave system is a three-lobed chamber known as Antro delle Sorti, the Cavern of the Fates, where the Praenestine oracle is supposed to have operated.

The other major oracle of Fortuna in Roman times was at Antium, now called Anzio. Both shrines are situated at the same latitude: Palastrina at 41°52'N and Anzio at 41°30'N. In pagan Rome were many smaller urban temples to Fortuna, who was worshipped under various epithets that dedicated her to most aspects of human and animal life. Many of these are listed on page 22.

Fig. 2.3. Mosaic of fish in the Cavern of Fates.
(Photograph by Camelia Boban)

EPITHETS OF FORTUNA

Fortuna Aucupium	Bird of Prey
Fortuna Augusta	Majestic
Fortuna Balnearis	Bathing
Fortuna Bona	Good
Fortuna Brevis	Short
Fortuna Conservatrix	Conservative
Fortuna Dubia	Doubts
Fortuna Equestris	Horseback Riding
Fortuna Felix	Happy
Fortuna Gubernans	Governing
Fortuna Liberum	Freedom
Fortuna Mala	Bad
Fortuna Mobilis	Movement
Fortuna Muliebris	Women
Fortuna Navirilis	Born
Fortuna Obsequens	Obeying
Fortuna Patricia	Noble
Fortuna Plebis	of the People
Fortuna Primigenia	Originiality
Fortuna Privata	Private
Fortuna Publica	Public
Fortuna Redux	Back
Fortuna Respiciens	Looking Back
Fortuna Restitutrix	Restorer
Fortuna Romana	Romans
Fortuna Salutaris	Saluting
Fortuna Tranquilla	Calm
Fortuna Virginalis	Purity, Chastity
Fortuna Virilis	Masculine

Fig. 2.4. The goddess Fortuna with spinning wheel
in one hand and a palm branch in the other,
illustrated by Hans Sebald Beham, 1541.
(Courtesy of Yellow Lion)

In Rome, the emperor Trajan (98–117 CE) dedicated a major temple to each aspect of the goddess, and on every January 1, offerings were made at the temples to ensure good luck and success for the coming year.

Like the oracle at Dodona in Greece, the oracle at Praeneste was believed to have been founded by an Egyptian priestess of Isis who went to Europe as a missionary, and the oracle was set up officially by Servius Tullius, the sixth king of Rome. Oracles of Fortuna were generally consulted for divination purposes by the drawing of lots: that is, dice or their equivalents. The Praenestine oracle used cubes of olive wood on which alphabetic characters were written. The cubes were thrown into a silver bowl and drawn out one by one to produce a sequence of letters that were taken as the first letters of words. Interpretative skill depended upon determining what the sequence of letters stood for with regard to the question asked or the person asking it.

Although the shrine may have been of Egyptian origin, the practice of using dice in divination in this context may have been Etruscan, and such Etruscan divination with letters may also have been the source from which runic divination was derived (Pennick 1990, 26). The Praenestine oracle had the ability to give readings in beautiful and disastrous detail, and it had a vogue in France in the early nineteenth century, when it was claimed that Charles Le Clerc used the oracle to attain prophecies for Napoleon Bonaparte. According to Herman Kirchenhoffer who published *The Book of Fate* in 1822, a list existed of Napoleon's questions to the oracle and its answers. Among them, he quotes several questions.

Napoleon: What is the aspect of the seasons and what political changes are likely to take place?

Oracle: A conqueror of noble mind and mighty power shall spring from low condition; he will break the chains of the oppressed and give liberty to the nations.

Another question,

Napoleon: Will my name be immortalized and will posterity applaud it?

Oracle: Abuse not the power which the Lord giveth thee, and thy name will be hailed with rapture in future ages. (Kirchenhoffer, quoted in Deacon 1977, 15–16)

Today, the goddess Fortuna is often called Lady Luck, a name that emerged in the twentieth century. She appears in the American magical tradition in preparations used by gamblers, who invoke her in the hope that they will win in games of chance. One New Orleans practice is to burn a specially prepared Lady Luck vigil candle during the waxing of the moon, praying for what one wishes and reciting the 23rd psalm (usually associated with funerals). The packaging of a contemporary American vigil candle dedicated to Lady Luck depicts her with numerous attributes of luck. In gambling advertisements, she is seen as a redhead, indicating the luck of the Irish, and she holds a four-leafed shamrock in her right hand and a left-handed adjustable spanner ("monkey wrench") in her left. She wears dice earrings, a horseshoe tiara, and a rabbit-foot key chain, and black eight balls cover her breasts. She wears a garter with a wishbone and a red dress with black card-suit sigils upon it, and she stands in front of a large horseshoe that uncharacteristically has eight instead of seven nail holes. In the four corners surrounding Lady Luck and the horseshoe are the four card-suit sigils.

HISTORIC DICE AND NUMBERS

Along with cowrie shells, bones are the most ancient form of divination. Astragali, the knuckle bones of sheep and similar ungulates, are the earliest known form of dice. They were used for divination in ancient Europe before the invention of the cubic die, which was also made from bone. There are southern African divination techniques using bone or wood tablets, which have

Fig. 2.5. Postcard, c.1900. Dice read three
unexpected things with a good outcome.
(Nigel Pennick Collection)

sometimes been called dice by colonial observers and anthropologists, for they serve the same function: to produce a randomized reading that can be attributed to agencies other than human.

Of ancient Egyptian dice, John Ashton wrote,

The bones used in gambling were, generally, those of sheep; but the Astragals of the antelope were much prized on account of their superior elegance. They also had regular dice, numbered like ours, which have been found at Thebes and elsewhere. (Ashton 1898, 4)

Fig. 2.6. Knucklebones is the generic term for astragali, which generally were from sheep (or goats), but others from different animals work in the same way.

The ancient Greek dice oracle of Termessos, located just inside the gatehouse of that walled city, used a randomized system to determine answers to questions. Seven astragali were thrown to generate numbers that corresponded to a particular verse that was inscribed on the wall of the shrine and provided answers to the queries posed.

Until the middle of the twentieth century, the power of the church in education in Britain was so great that the primary historical reference of writers, politicians, and the judiciary was the Bible. The society and mores of the ancient Jews were taken as the recommended model for society's action in the present day, and hence writers on divination and gambling frequently cited

Fig. 2.7. Wooden divination plaques, Mashona, Southern Zimbabwe.
(Courtesy of the Wellcome Collection)

ancient Jewish practice in their works. For example, in 1898
John Ashton wrote:

> As far as we know, the ancient Jews did not gamble except
> by drawing, or casting lots; and as we find no word against it
> in the inspired writings, and, as even one of the apostles was
> chosen by lot (Acts I, 26), it must be assumed that this form
> of gambling meets with the divine approval. We are not told
> how the lots were drawn; but the casting of lots pre-supposes
> the use of dice, and this seems to have been practiced from
> very early times, for we find in Leviticus XVI 8, that "Aaron
> shall cast lots upon the two goats; one lot for the Lord, and
> the other lot for the scape goat." And the promised land was
> expressly and divinely ordained to be divided by an appeal to
> chance. Numbers XXVI, 52 and 55, 56, "And the Lord spake
> unto Moses, saying. . . . Notwithstanding the land shall be
> divided by lot; according to the names of the tribes of their

Fig. 2.8. The Pergamum bowl used by the ancient Greeks for divination. (Drawing by Nigel Pennick)

fathers they shall inherit. According to the lot shall the possession thereof be divided between many and few." The reader can find very many more references to the use of the "lot" in any concordance of the Bible. (Ashton 1898, 4–5)

Of course the ancient Jews used divination, or lots, to allocate the land they had just occupied in Canaan. But the Jews were not the only ancient tribe or nation that used this random way to allocate land or choose which animal should be sacrificed to the gods. Writers whose primary source was biblical naturally put the origin of lots in this ancient Hebrew practice, but this assertion is only an artefact of the bibliocentric worldview in education that prevailed at the time and a lack of recognition that the practices in the Bible are only one set of cultural activities that pertained to one particular ancient religious group.

But the importance placed on the biblical text meant that it was used as the standard by which all else was judged. Appendix 1 of this book is an example of this with regard to divination in Elizabethan England, where all manner of lots and gambling are discussed using the Bible as the authority to condemn it. Of course, all across the world divination existed and exists that had no connection whatever with biblical Judaism. Divination was certainly practiced in Egypt millennia before Judaism emerged as a coherent religion and the Jews as a discrete tribal ethnicity, and related African traditions flourish today.

Ashton states that gambling was looked down upon in ancient Rome and

> the term *aleator* [dicer], or gambler, was one of reproach and many were the edicts against it: utterly useless, of course, but it was allowed during the Saturnalia. Money lost at play could not be legally recovered by the winner, and money paid by the loser might by him be recovered from the person who had won and received the same. (Ashton 1898, 6–7)

According to Ashton, the emperor Augustus was a passionate dice player, as was Nero.

> Caligula, after a long spell of ill-luck, in which he had lost all his money, rushed into the streets, had two innocent Roman knights seized, and ordered their goods to be confiscated. Whereupon he returned to his game, remarking that this had been the luckiest throw he had had for a long time. Claudius

had his carriages arranged for dicing convenience, and wrote a work on the subject. (Ashton 1898, 12)

While dice are the preeminent gambling system, they may have originated in divination as discussed earlier. The art of divining the future through the usage of throwing dice is known as cleromancy, astragalomancy, or psephomancy. The word *die* is etymologically derived from the Old French *dé* and from the Latin *datum,* meaning "that which is given," inferring an oracle or ostentum given by the gods. The word *die* is used generally to mean the cubic, six-sided die that has always been its most common form. The plural of die is dice, but people often use the plural to describe a single die as "a dice."

The numbers on dice have their own names. Roman dice terminology was related to the twelvefold division of the world, as expressed in weights and measures such as the twelvefold division of length into the twelve inches in the foot (Kretschmer, 5–6). The following table provides length measurement equivalents of the points on the die:

ROMAN MEASUREMENTS REPRESENTED ON A DIE

NUMBER OF POINTS	ROMAN NAME	INCHES	PART OF A FOOT
1	Uncia	one inch	one-twelfth of a foot
2	Sextans	two inches	one-sixth of a foot
3	Quadrans	three inches	one-quarter of a foot
4	Triens	four inches	one-third of a foot
5	Quincunx	five inches	five-twelfths of a foot
6	Semis	six inches	half a foot

Contemporary names for one, two, and three on a die are ace, deuce, and tray, though there are, inevitably, many variations that one may encounter. Slim Gaillard's 1940s jive talk *Vout-O-Reenee Dictionary* numbers one to twelve as "ake, theu, few, raw, tiff, ax, effa, octa, nie, ake-thee, ake-ake, ake-theu." In American craps, two ones are called snake eyes or snake's eyes, and two sixes are boxcars, after the standard American railway van.

Although the word *die* is generally used to mean a six-sided cubic die, solid geometry allows many other forms, but they are more difficult to make. Four-sided oracular dice were used in the Indian dice oracle or game called Pāśaka-kēvalī, which used three tetrahedral dice thrown onto a cloth. There are only eighteen combinations of this kind of die from one-one-one to four-four-four, the numbers being the first four letters of the alphabet, but the fall of the dice on particular divisions of the divining cloth gave sixty-four possible readings.

Fig. 2.9. Modern set of multisided dice.
(Courtesy of Official URL)

A similar tetrahedral dice divination system called Fal Nameh was used by the Turks of the Ottoman Empire. Twelve-sided dice appeared in France in a 1556 work by François Grujet. Renaissance improvements in geometrical technique had by then enabled the physical production of such complex geometrical forms. In the late twentieth century, the popularity of military and fantasy role-playing games combined with the technical expertise for making multisided dice meant that they became commonplace, and although comparable gambling games using them have not developed to any extent, a twenty-sided die is used in the modern Magic 8 Ball divination system.

Divination, or the invocation of random external forces, has been used in significant matters for a very long time. The oracle book the *I Ching* was used in warfare by generals in China from

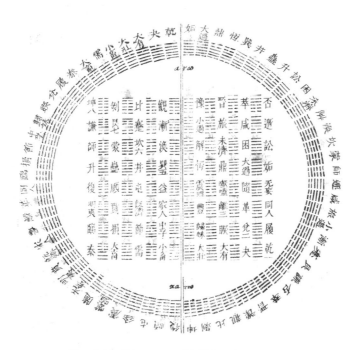

Fig. 2.10. Diagram of I Ching hexagrams
owned by Gottfried Wilhelm Leibniz, 1701.

the fifth century BCE to the twentieth century CE regardless of the ideological cause for which they were fighting. King Kou Chien-chih (fifth century BCE), Chu-ko Liang (181–234 CE), Chiang Kai-shek (1887–1975) and Mao Zedong (Mao Tse-tung, 1893–1976) all employed the *I Ching*. The last two, who were opponents in China's last civil war, which ended in 1949, demonstrate that if both sides in a conflict refer to the same powers, one must still lose.

3

DIVINATORY GEOMANCY
....
Creating Figures for Readings

ivinatory geomancy is an ancient form of divination inti-
mately connected to divination by dice. Figures are produced by mathematical means that have specific meanings that
are interpreted in the light of an original question posed at the
beginning of the procedure. Divinatory geomancy uses a number
of binary choices that are combined to create symbolic figures that
either have a meaning within themselves or reference a text or verse
in an oral tradition or an oracle book. The well-known Chinese
I Ching and the ancient Greek oracle of Termessos, both mentioned
in the previous chapter, belong to the latter category. Those who
consult the *I Ching* randomly select stalks of the yarrow plant to
produce figures that refer to specific texts in the book, while users of
the oracle of Termessos looked to the fall of astragali to determine
the verses that would provide the answers to their questions.

Undoubtedly, originally this sacred knowledge was transmitted
orally and was systematized into oracle books when it was deemed

they should be written down and thereby made unchangeable. The common way of remembering divinatory texts in Africa is by verses that can be transmitted orally, like songs. In some instances, this traditional way is still in existence, though certain texts considered definitive may have been recorded by outside researchers. For example, the verses of the Ifá sixteen cowries divination in West Africa were orally transmitted until 1951, when William and Berta Bascom recorded the Orishala priest and diviner Salako reciting the entire corpus of verses on tape (Bascom 1980, 3–14). Like all forms of divination, divinatory geomancy is a ritualized means of obtaining otherwise inaccessible information, which is then brought into the realm of everyday existence in order to solve problems or enable the querent to formulate a plan of action. The ritual nature of divination separates it from everyday human interactions and conflicts by means of the intervention of another way of knowing.

Divinatory geomancy is essentially a binary system. The figures are composed of four lines, each of which may be an odd or even number, conventionally one or two points, respectively. The four lines are arranged vertically, called from top to bottom head, neck, body, and feet. There are sixteen possible combinations, each with a name and meaning. The lines are generated randomly. Traditionally they have been calculated by making marks at random on the earth or in sand or casting seeds, stones, or shells and then counting them to produce either an odd or even outcome. Some West African diviners use a chain that has elements that can fall upward or downward. Similarly, two coins can be tossed, with two heads or two tails representing an even outcome, and a head and a tail an odd one. A single die will give either an odd or even number, dominoes can be turned over at random, and various packs of geomancy cards have been produced occasionally.

Fig. 3.1. Ikin Orossi divination table of the Ifá.

Geomancy is in the area of expertise of the "root doctor," for roots and vegetables that grow in the ground are ideal means of generating geomantic figures. There are techniques that use the roots of mandrake and black bryony and involve counting the knobs and rootlets, but as these are scarce, other more plentiful roots are usually used.

An East Anglian technique for generating odd and even sequences uses potatoes. Each potato is different, for each has an indeterminate number of eyes, the places from which new growth takes place. To generate a geomantic figure, one must take four potatoes at random and count the eyes on each one. Odd or even numbers are reduced in the same way that dots or scribes at random become geomantic figures. The number of eyes of the first potato gives the bottom line of the figure—its *feet*. The second potato gives the second line from the bottom, the *body;* the third gives the third line, or *neck;* and the fourth gives the top line, or *head*. The procedure is repeated four times to create the *mothers*, as in divinatory geomancy. Thus it requires sixteen potatoes.

It is likely that geomantic divination originated in Africa, and it is clear that a form of it was practiced in ancient Egypt four thousand years ago, for the cowrie-shell girdles worn by women in the Middle Kingdom were strikingly similar to the chains of cowrie shells used in present-day divination in West Africa. The Opele Ifá divining chain is made from eight pairs of cowrie shells or half seed pods linked with a double line of chain. The cowrie shells and pods have a concave and a convex face, which gives two possible readings when thrown. The diviner holds the chain in the middle with four shells or pods hanging on each side. Then it is thrown so that it falls in two parallel rows, and the faces turn up giving four odd or even readings.

An ancient Egyptian cowrie-shell belt made of gold is preserved in the Metropolitan Museum of Art in New York. It was taken from the tomb of Princess Sit-Hathor-Yunet, a daughter of King Sesostris II, who reigned from 1878 to 1843 BCE. Another such belt, belonging to Queen Mereret, also composed of eight golden replicas of cowrie shells, was preserved in the Cairo Museum.

The sixteen geomantic figures were known in the system called *raml* in the early Arab Empire across North Africa and the Middle East, where they acquired Arabic names and correspondences from Islamic spiritual traditions. Mediterranean Jewish practitioners called it the science of points, or Hokhma Ha-Nekudot and "the lot by sand," or Goral Ha-Goralot. Jewish geomantic divination was recorded in a text called *Sepher Ha-Goralot*.

Geomantic divination appears to have been transmitted northward into Europe through Morocco and Islamic Spain, entering the repertoire of Christian monastic scribes. The oldest recognized European texts on divinatory geomancy are *Ars geomantiae* and

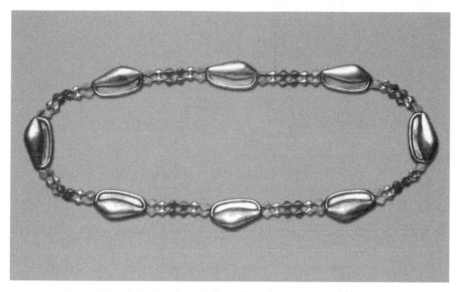

Fig. 3.2. Cowrie shell girdle of Sithathoryunet,
the daughter of Pharaoh Senusret II, of the 12th dynasty.
(Courtesy of the Metropolitan Museum of Art)

Geomantia nova, written in Aragon by Hugh of Santalla around the year 1140.

The technique spread through western Europe through the works of Gerard of Cremona (1114–1187), Plato of Tivoli, who was a contemporary of Hugh of Santalla, Michael Scot (c. 1175–c. 1235), and Albertus Magnus (1193–1280). Coming into Europe from the monotheistic Muslims, geomancy did not acquire a reputation of being pagan and thus demonic and hence was little condemned. The theologian Thomas Aquinas taught in his Quodlibet that Christians were allowed to practice geomantic divination because it is part of astrology, being reckoned as the "daughter of astrology."

The sixteen geomantic figures used in the European version of this divination are given Latin names. These names and descriptions of the figures' meanings and planetary, astrological, and elemental correspondences are provided in the list below.

I. Via (*Iter,* "journey"), The Way—signifies a path, street, road, journey, direction in life, ways and means. It is generally a neutral figure, though it affects other figures unfavorably. However, when the question involves travel, it is favorable. Via corresponds to the water element, the Moon, and the zodiac sign of Cancer, the crab. Its fortunate time is Monday night.

II. Acquisitio (*Comprehensum intus,* "understood within"), Gain—Signifies acquisition, gain, profit, success, and great benefit. It is a good figure, corresponding to the fire element, Jupiter, and Sagittarius. Its fortunate day is Thursday.

III. Puella (*Mundus facie,* "immaculate face"), The Girl— Signifies a girl, daughter, young wife, pleasant character, cleanliness, and purity. Ostensibly a beneficial figure, Puella may mean that good outer appearances may conceal less pleasant things. Puella corresponds to Venus and Libra, and its element is air. Its fortunate times are Monday and Friday nights.

IV. Conjunctio (*Collectio,* "collection"), Union—Signifies connection, gathering together, collection, reunion, recovery of lost things, and contracts. It is on the positive side of neutral. Conjunctio corresponds to the earth element, Mercury, and Virgo. The nights of Wednesday and Saturday are its best times.

V. Tristitia (*Diminutus,* "diminished"), Sadness—Signifies the downside of all things: sadness, misery, melancholy, blame, humiliation, diminution, diminishing resources, poverty, cross purposes, and a change for the worse. It corresponds to Saturn, Aquarius, and the element of air. Its best day is Saturday.

VI. Albus (*Candidus,* "bright"), White—Signifies whiteness, illumination, wisdom, dazzling beauty, clarity of thought, and good results in business. It is an overall positive figure. Albus corresponds to Mercury, Gemini, and the element of air. Its best days are Wednesday and Saturday.

VII. **Caput Draconis** (*Limen Intrans*, "crossing the threshold"), The Dragon's Head—Signifies the interior threshold, the astrological Dragon's Head (the ascending node of the Moon), a doorway to the upperworld. It is a good figure, corresponding to Jupiter and Venus. Its sign is Capricorn, and its element is earth. The fortunate days of Caput Draconis are Thursday and Friday.

VIII. **Fortuna Major** (*Tutela Intrans*, "entering protection"), The Greater Fortune—Signifies good luck, success, good fortune, victory, safe property, assistance from within, a good position in society, and inner protection. It is an extremely good figure. It corresponds to the Sun, Leo, and element of fire. The best day is Sunday.

IX. **Fortuna Minor** (*Tutela Extrans*, "emergent guardian"), The Lesser Fortune—Signifies assistance from others and protection from harm coming from outside. It is a reasonably beneficial figure, but far less so than Fortuna Major. Like Fortuna Major, it corresponds to the Sun, Leo, and its element is fire. Its fortunate times are Thursday noon and Saturday night.

X. **Cauda Draconis** (*Limen Exiens*, "exiting the threshold"), The Dragon's Tail—Signifies the exterior threshold, the astrological Dragon's Tail (the descending node of the Moon), a way out, possible problems, and the underworld. It is a bad figure, corresponding with Mars and Saturn, Scorpio, and the element of fire. Its operative day in Tuesday.

XI. **Rubeus,** Red—Signifies bloodshed, passion, bad temper, viciousness, destructive energies, fire, and general danger. It is a sign to stop a divination. It corresponds with Mars and Scorpio, but its element is water. It is most powerful on Tuesday and Friday night.

XII. **Laetitia** (*Ridens,* "laughing"), Joy—Signifies joy, gladness, delight, beauty, grace, balance, sanity, good health, and matters concerning the head. It is a very good figure. It corresponds with Jupiter, Pisces, and the element of water. Its fortunate days are Sunday and Thursday.

XIII. **Carcer,** The Prison—Signifies a prison, confinement, servitude, fetters, hindrance, binding, and delay. Depending on the question, its significance is either good or bad. Its fortunate times are Wednesday night and Saturday.

XIV. **Puer** (Gladius Erigendus), The Boy—Signifies a boy, a son, a servant, an employee, the erect phallus, a sword, combativeness, inconsiderateness, and rashness. Puer is a negative figure in all questions but those concerning combat or love. It is ruled by Mars and Aries, and its element is fire. Puer's best day is Tuesday.

XV. **Amissio** (Comprehensum Extus), Loss—Signifies exterior comprehension, things that are taken away, loss through illness, theft of property, and financial problems. Amissio is a bad figure, corresponding with Venus, Taurus, and the element of earth. Its powerful day is Friday.

XVI. **Populus** (Congregatio), The People—Signifies the people, a crowd, an assembly, a gang, a congregation, a state of freedom, and the common people as opposed to the ruling class. It has a changeable quality, depending on the meaning of the other figures in the reading. It corresponds with the Moon, Cancer, and the element of water. Its good times are Monday and Thursday night.

The sixteen geomantic figures can be grouped in opposing pairs; some possess complementary meanings and some opposing

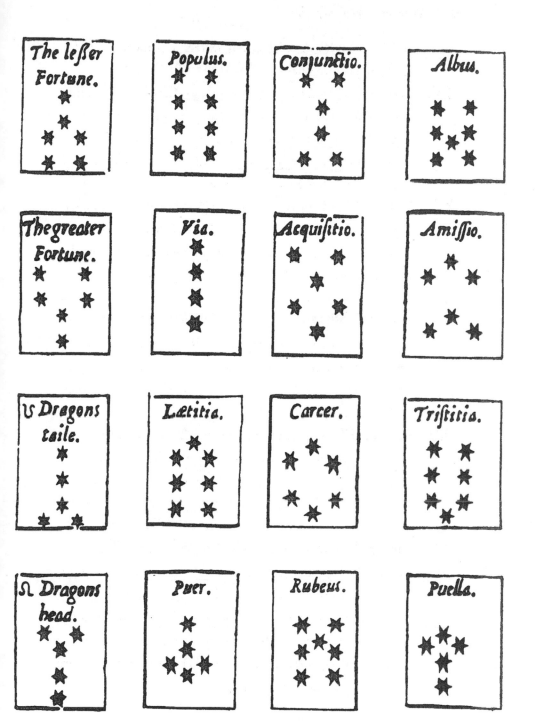

Fig. 3.3. The sixteen figures of divinatory geomancy, 17th century.
(Nigel Pennick Collection)

GEOMANTIC FIGURES
GROUPED IN OPPOSING PAIRS

POPULUS (XVI)	VIA (I)
• •	•
• •	•
• •	•
• •	•

TRISTITIA (V)	LAETITIA (XII)
• •	•
• •	• •
• •	• •
•	• •

FORTUNA MAJOR (VIII)	FORTUNA MINOR (IX)
• •	•
• •	•
•	• •
•	• •

ACQUISITIO (II)	AMISSIO (XV)
• •	•
•	• •
• •	•
•	• •

CARCER (XIII)	CONJUNCTIO (IV)
•	• •
• •	•
• •	•
•	• •

PUELLA (III)	PUER (XIV)
•	•
• •	•
•	• •
•	•

ALBUS (VI)	RUBEUS (XI)
• •	• •
• •	•
•	• •
• •	• •

CAPUT DRACONIS (VII)	CAUDA DRACONIS (X)
• •	•
•	•
•	•
•	• •

Like runes, some geomantic figures are noninvertible (that is, they look the same whichever way up they appear). The inversion of other figures, however, produces their opposite or complementary form and meaning as with Puer and Puella, Caput Draconis and Cauda Draconis, Fortuna Major and Fortuna Minor, Albus and Rubeus, Acquisitio and Amissio, and Tristitia and Laetitia.

The technique of geomantic divination is twofold: firstly, the random system used produces a series of odd and even numbers from which are created four preliminary figures; then from these four figures, additional figures are derived. From this final set of figures, the reading is taken.

The querent begins by casting the points either by making a random number of marks in a row without conscious effort or counting, but fewer than twenty in whatever direction one is used to writing: in sand or on paper, by tossing seeds, shells, dice, or coins, or by using a divining chain or potatoes. The chosen method is done sixteen times, and each time the numbers are counted to determine either an odd or even outcome. Only oddness or evenness matters—any odd number is reduced to a single dot in a figure's line, and any even one, to two dots. The first four outcomes make the first geomantic figure, the south figure. The next four make the second, east, figure; the third, the north figure, and the fourth is the west figure. These original four geomantic figures are the mothers. They are drawn at the top right of the diagram called the *geomantic shield* that is prepared beforehand to record the figures.

From these four mothers, four more figures called the *daughters* are made by recombination. The head (top row) of the first daughter is the point or points that compose the head (top row) of the first/south, mother. The neck of the first daughter is made from the head of the second/east mother; the body of the first daughter is made from the points of the head of the third/north mother; and the feet of the first daughter are made from the point or points composing the head of the fourth/west mother. This procedure is repeated to make the additional three daughters. The second daughter is composed of the necks (second rows) of the four mothers, the third daughter from the bodies (third row) of the four mothers, and the fourth daughter from the feet (bottom row) of the four mothers, added in the same sequence as the first daughter.

After the four daughters have been formed, a further four figures are constructed. These are the nephews. They are made from the mothers and the daughters by adding the corresponding rows of pairs. The first nephew is made by adding the corresponding rows of the first two mothers together. For example, if the heads (top row) of the first two mothers add up to an odd number, the head of the first nephew will be a single point; if they add up to an even number, the nephew's head will be two points. The neck, body, and feet of the first nephew are determined by adding the corresponding rows of the first two mothers in the same way. The second nephew is formed by the addition of the second two mothers. The third and fourth nephews are created by adding together the points of the first two daughters for the third nephew and the second two daughters for the fourth nephew.

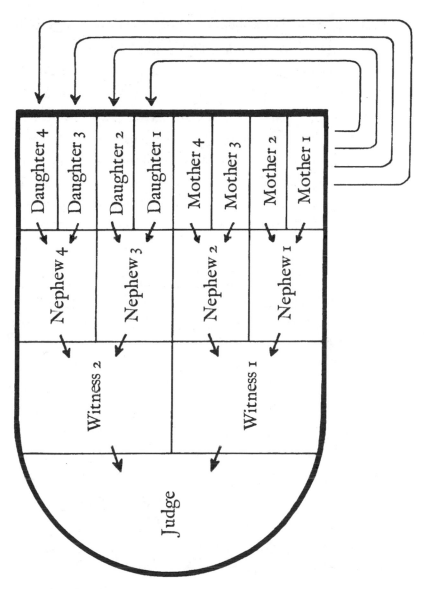

Fig. 3.4. Erecting the Geomantic Chart.
(Diagram by Nigel Pennick)

The next figures to be made are the two witnesses. These are made by adding points of pairs of nephews in the same way as the previous figures are made. The first witness is formed from the points of the first and second nephews; the second witness from the third and fourth nephews. Finally, the two witnesses are added to make the judge. The mathematics of divinatory geomancy means that the judge can only be one of eight possible figures, Via (I), Acquisitio (II), Conjunctio (IV), Fortuna Major (VIII), Fortuna Minor (IX), Carcer (XIII), Amissio (XV), and Populus (XVI). The judge gives the final answer to the question posed at the start of the divination. In most cases, it appears unequivocal, but, should the meaning be uncertain, a deciding figure, the reconciler, can be made by adding the points of the first mother and the judge.

THE PRODUCTION OF
GEOMANTIC FIGURES—FORTUNA MINOR (IX)

ROW	POSITION	RANDOM POINTS	ODD OR EVEN	GEOMANTIC FIGURE
1	Head	• • • • • • •	Odd	•
2	Neck	• • • • •	Odd	•
3	Body	• • • • • •	Even	• •
4	Feet	• • • • • • • • •	Even	• •

EXAMPLE OF THE ADDITION
OF FIGURES' ROWS

CONJUNCTIO (IV)	PUER (XIV)	RANDOM POINTS	ODD OR EVEN	PUELLA (III)
• •	•	• • •	Odd	•
•	•	• •	Even	• •
•	• •	• • •	Odd	•
• •	•	• • •	Odd	•

The binary principle of odd or even is continued throughout the adding process to produce the final figure, the judge.

THE *SANCTORUM SORTES*

Dice Divination

EUROPEAN ORACLE BOOKS

One of the oldest oracle books of the Christian era in Europe was the Latin *Sortes apostolorum,* which was attributed to St. Matthias. This was considered heretical in some quarters, for in the year 465 the Church Council of Vannes banned *Sanctorum sortes,* which is the class of divination through which the *Sortes apostolorum* operates. This may well have been a dice oracle using three dice, giving fifty-six possible readings, for a tenth-century manuscript of the *Sortes apostolorum* operated through readings for three dice (Götze 1918, 4). In these religious oracle books, appropriate aphorisms or prayers were given as answers to the question posed. In thirteenth-century Germany, oracle books known as *lôgbuochen* were banned (Götze 1918, 9). Large parts of what is now eastern Germany were

8

No. 4. How many suitors shall I have?

6	7	9	1	1	3	1
N	F	6	2	T	1	2
2	4	T	3	2	T	1
11	3	T	N	T	1	5
1	T	3	4	1	T	2
2	3	N	2	5	6	5
4	1	1	3	1	2	3
2	3	2	2	T	T	T
1	1	T	3	2	5	4

N, none—T, treacherous lovers.

5. How many houses shall I have of my own?

N	P	3	50	1	2	5
1	2	5	P	11	13	2
1	26	40	7	16	1	3
10	30	50	100	P	P	15
9	35	N	1	P	N	14
P	12	30	33	35	100	N

N, none—P, prison.

9

6. How many pounds is the most I shall ever possess at one time?

6	1	10	15	3	50
N	12	N	N	21	6
35	7	70	10,000	1	4
5	1	100	50	100	8
5	4	10,000	5	3	2
1	20	3	21	1	6
50	N	4	5	6	100
N	78	3	2	1	9

Figures for pounds, and N for none.

No. 7. How many miles shall I travel?

1000	F	1	2	3	1
S	1	10,000	2	F	S
3	2	9	3	4	6	S
24	30	5	5	7	1	3
5	6	2	4	6	4	1
10	11	3	15	7	9	2
3	5	20	100	1	4	50

N, none—S, sea—F, foreign land.

Fig. 4.1. Pages from *The Real Bergami Fortune Teller* oracle book, circa 1800. "By Cornelia, the famous sybil, who foretold the good fortune and exaltation of Baron Bergami, in which twelve questions on the important subjects of love and marriage are truly answered. To which is added, Charms, ceremonies, dreams, etc." (Courtesy Cleveland Public Library)

pagan at the time, and the church organized crusades to override and exterminate the Indigenous faith there.

The use of runes and other forms of traditional divination by the Old Prussians and other eastern Germanic and Slavonic peoples clearly had some influence upon the contents of the *lôgbuochen*. But in German-speaking lands in the late medieval period when the Christian church had succeeded in destroying pagan religion were texts called *Losbücher* that contained ostensibly religious or secular texts that could be consulted as oracles to provide answers to problems. Some were very ornate and contained a spinner that could be used to point to particular emblems or sigils that provided the answer to the question posed.

In his 1918 commentary on *Das strassburger würfelbuch* (The Strasbourg Dice Book, 1529), Alfred Götze mentions fifteenth-century French dice oracles that had 232 corresponding answers to rolls of the dice. An Italian divination book by Lorenzo Spirito, titled *Delle Sorti,* was published in Perugia in 1482. It dealt with divination by dice and the wheel of fortune. Subsequently it was condemned as superstitious in the French denunciatory work of 1581, *De la démonomanie des sorciers.*

In 1527 a two-dice oracle book by Sigismondo Fanti appeared in Ferrara, Italy. A German oracle text of 1473, which uses three cubic dice as in the *Sanctorum sortes,* also had spiritual principles underlying the fifty-six readings. The dice roll one, one, one has as its text a rhyme attributed to Satan, concerning falling into superstition and the belief in magic (Götze 1918, 10). This throw is the three-dice equivalent of snake's eyes in the two-dice crap game. Unlike in present-day literalist superstition, Satan was not allied with triple six, the equivalent of boxcars in craps.

The German scribe Konrad Mulitor wrote ten divination books in Bavaria between 1450 and 1473. Four were for divination by dice. Mulitor's third book deals with divinations on complexion and nature, while his fourth book is an oracle that has fifty-six verses telling of one's good luck and bad luck, faithfulness, and falsehood in love (Götze 1918, 10–11).

An early printed book on divination with three dice is Das strassburger würfelbuch. The city of Strasbourg, where it was

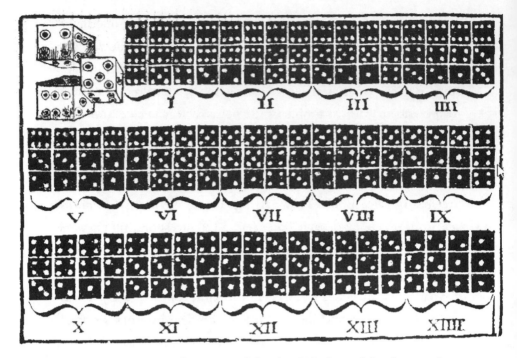

Fig. 4.2. *Das strassburger würfelbuch,* 1529. One of the first oracle
books to deal with divination by dice.
(Nigel Pennick Collection)

published in 1529, was then called Strassburg and was a German-
speaking city of the Holy Roman Empire. Now it is part of France.

The text of *Das strassburger würfelbuch* is divided into fourteen sections, each with four combinations—fifty-six in all. In section I, which deals with the throws that produce three 6s, 6-6-5,
6-6-4, and 6-6-3. Section II has the throws 6-6-2, 6-6-1, 6-5-5, and
6-5-4. Section III commences with 6-5-3, and the combinations
continue with diminishing scores until section XIIII ends with
1-1-1. Each combination is accompanied by a four-line doggerel
rhyme that tells the given divinatory meaning of the combination.

Some of the dice books have texts that refer to themes in
the *Narrenliteratur* texts that circulated (and circulate today) at
carnival time, dealing with stupidity, drunkenness, gluttony, and

so on. These themes also appear in the carnivalesque imagery of Sebastian Brant's 1494 book, *Das Narrenschiff* (*The Ship of Fools*). Other versions of the same theme are mythical lands of idleness and plenty (or sloth and gluttony), Schlaraffenland, the Land of Cokaygne, or Luilekkerland and the twentieth-century American version, The Big Rock Candy Mountain.

In Strasbourg in 1539 appeared Jörg Wickram's dice-based *Orakel der Liebe,* and in the same city in 1546 another dice book by Balthasar Beck appeared, which, like *Das strassburger würfelbuch* also used three dice. A 1556 French work by François Gruget titled *Le plaisant jeu du dodechedron de fortune* used special twelve-sided dice. *Le panthéon et temple des oracles* by François d'Hervé (1625) was another version of the Strasbourg system using three standard cubic dice (Götze 1918, 8–9).

Some German *Losbücher* had a spinner that was used as a means of fortune-telling with a pointer that randomly indicated a particular emblem and text that provided the answer to the question posed. In England, George Wither's *Collection of Emblemes* of 1635 also used this technique. It consisted of emblematic engravings taken from a 1611 Dutch emblem book to which Wither added rhyming texts he had written.

Although he was religiously a Puritan, *Emblemes* was a book that Wither called a *lotterie:* that is, an oracle or fortune-telling book. There was a dial with fifty-six numbers, selected by an arrow on a spinner, while another was at the center of a diagram divided into the Four Winds. The East Wind corresponded to the text of the first "booke," the South to the second, the West to the third, and the North to the fourth. The querent first spun the dial to get a number, then spun the Four Winds spinner to determine which of the four books the number was in. This gave 224 possible results. Wither described the means of using his book as follows: with closed eyes, the querent had to spin the arrow once for a page number and then again to discover in which of the Four Winds (bookes) the text was to be found. Although it was a very expensive book, it was popular, for various editions of it were produced (there was no copyright in that time), and new editions were appearing until the 1720s.

CONTEMPORARY DICE GAMES

All of the oracular systems that use dice are based on the scores of individual dice; they do not work on the scores of all dice added together. Consequently, the odds of any particular combination turning up are not the same as those in dice games, more like scoring the hard way in craps. The divinatory three-dice roll is the basis of the modern gambling game called buck dice. The object of the game is to score fifteen points called the "buck," and each player who scores it in turn drops out until the last player who has not reached the score of fifteen remains. This is the loser who must pay up.

Related to buck dice is a gambling device called the Big Six Wheel or Jumbo Dice Wheel, also called the Wheel of Fortune, referring to the attribute of the goddess Fortuna. This is a wheel that is around five feet in diameter, mounted on a horizontal axis so it spins in the vertical plane—unlike a roulette wheel, which spins in the horizontal. Around the rim are fifty-four spaces that show three dice in each space, each having a different combination. The wheel is spun clockwise, and pegs on the outside of the wheel click as they pass by a tab at the top, which indicates the dice combination when the wheel stops. Gamblers bet on a layout that gives them odds lower than the true odds of the particular combinations, and, in addition, there are two combinations missing from the wheel, which, to be fair, should have fifty-six. Some versions of the Big Six have even fewer sections, giving the gambling house an even better percentage take on each spin of the wheel.

CONTEMPORARY SIMPLE
DICE DIVINATION

As with all divination systems, every possible variant of dice system exists. It is up to the diviner to choose which system they like best. The old European oracle books are complex, and many people do not agree with the religious tone of the books or consider them obsolete, so far more simple techniques are favored by contemporary practitioners.

Two- or three-dice systems are most common, and the score rather than the actual combinations on the die matters most. This, of course, means that certain readings are more common than others, as the statistics of craps (two dice) and buck dice or chuck-a-luck (three dice) still apply even though they are not taken into account, as they must be with gamblers. Some dice diviners will roll the dice on a cloth or the floor and just take the score as the reading, while others draw a square or circle in which the dice are thrown. The square or circle is used to define the validity of a reading. Some see a die that falls outside the line as meaning the reading is aborted; others see such dice as having significance, such as predicting a future argument. Some people who use the square or circle give a meaning to the number of dice that cross the line. One die outside the line may signify future difficulties, two going over the line represents disagreements, while three (if used) outside the circle is considered a lucky sign, perhaps of a wish being fulfilled. Of course the outside-the-circle rule is a cheat's charter.

Suggested meanings of dice throws are often based on the numerology of "lucky numbers." The system listed below is one example. (Note: a throw of two is only available when two dice rather than three are used, and throws of thirteen through eighteen can only be scored when three dice are used.)

A NUMEROLOGY OF
LUCKY NUMBERS SYSTEM

2	Recommends that the querent should examine the situation carefully to avoid hidden difficulties.
3	Signifies unexpected things with a good outcome and transformative change.
4	Indicates hindrances, either from external circumstances or disagreements with other people.
5	Denotes unexpected assistance leading to successful outcomes.
6	Signifies bad luck and loss.
7	Indicates money problems and loss of reputation. Paradoxically, 7 is considered to be a lucky number, and this reading can also mean luck in love—the "unlucky with money, lucky in love" paradox.
8	Recommends delay, not making a decision in a hurry.
9	Signifies luck in gambling and love, a loving partnership, and prosperity.
10	Denotes new beginnings, birth, success in business, and monetary matters.
11	Suggests illness, parting, and possibly death.
12	Indicates the arrival of an important message involving a substantial sum of money.
13	The traditional unlucky number (remember Carcer, which is number XIII in geomantic divination and means confinement). Indicates an unhappy time, disappointment, and failure if the querent continues on the present course.
14	Signifies new things and new people in the querent's life.

15	Recommends caution and avoidance of other people's troubles.
16	Denotes a short trip or pleasant diversion away from everyday things.
17	Suggests that the querent's plans should be altered and others' advice should be heeded.
18	Signifies success, happiness, and an improvement in social status.

ROLL THEM LAUGHING BONES

·······································

The Dicer's Grip,
Controlled Shots, and Crooked Dice

THE CRAP GAME

The best throw of the dice is to throw them away.

ENGLISH PROVERB

The most common American dice game is craps. The origin of the name of the game is unknown, so there are a number of ingenious explanations for it, all of them more or less implausible. Some claim that in its early days, it was called by the French name *cra-paud,* meaning "frog" or "toad." Some suppose this to refer to the frog-like appearance of people crouched over the ground or floor on which the dice were thrown, though the toad-frog connection with gambling magic is part of the American hoodoo tradition (in the United States the amphibian is called a toad, in Britain is called a toad-frog).

In another version of the origin myth, the frog connection is suggested to come from its supposed origin in Louisiana when it was a French colony, through the national insult calling French people Johnny Crapaud (frog eater). Another related suggestion is that there was a street called Rue de Craps in New Orleans when it was French, and this gave the dice game its name. Yet another more plausible story says it comes from the English term *crabs* that was used in the game of hazard to signify a dice throw scoring two or three. Whatever the origin of its name, craps has a vast array of stories and legends associated with it. It is a whole culture in its own right.

The crap game uses a pair of standard cubic dice. Probability means that the most likely throw of two dice is a seven. If at first throw, a seven or eleven (a natural) is scored, the thrower wins and must throw again. If the first throw scores a two, three, or twelve (craps), the thrower has lost. But if the thrower scores a four, five,

Fig. 5.1. Craps game at U.S. military camp in 1918.
(Courtesy of Richard Arthur Norton)

six, eight, nine, or ten, that score becomes their point. Another throw follows where the thrower hopes to make their point again and win. But if they throw a seven, that is a loss, and the next player throws the dice. The other players make bets on the outcome of the thrower or side bets that the thrower will win. In casinos and gambling houses, all bets are made with the house, both for and against.

THE DICE CHEATS

The odds that certain numbers will turn up when two or more dice are thrown is fixed—so long as the dice are square and on the level and thrown in a fully random way. But this is easier said than done. When hand throwing a pair or three dice and cup throwing a number of dice, there are many ways of throwing them with controlled shots that maximize the chances that certain numbers will turn up. In dice play, there are well-known grips and kinds of shots that are intended not to produce a random result. Skewed, nonrandom outcomes are easier to achieve with hand-thrown dice, but even using dice cups, there are particular ways of holding and shaking that produce nonrandom results. These are in the domain of legerdemain, or prestidigitation, arts practiced by close-up stage magicians and con men. To perform these shots it is necessary not only to practice the movements, but also to learn another essential technique called setting, which is used by dice cheats and involves memorizing the orientations of dice that will produce the desired score when thrown deftly.

How old these grips and shots are is not recorded. However, the principles according to which they operate are simple, and it is inconceivable that they do not originate in the earliest days of dice divination and play. In his *History of Gambling in England*, John Ashton wrote:

Nor was it all fair play with those ancients. Aristotle already knows of a way by which the dice can be made to fall as the player wishes them; and even the cunningly constructed, turret-shaped dice cup did not prevent occasional "mendings" of luck. The Berlin Museum contains one "charged" die, and another with a double four. (Ashton 1898, 12)

In play, the purpose of grips and controlled shots is to skew the odds in favor of the thrower: that is, to cheat the ostensibly random nature of the game. In ancient dice oracles where a priest-ess or priest threw the dice at the behest of a question, it is not unlikely that on some occasions one or another of these particular grips and shots was used either to eliminate certain potential read-ings or to produce others.

The easiest grip to play with, and the first one a would-be dice cheat learns is the lock grip. The thrower holds the pair of dice in their hand and shakes them seemingly to randomize the throw. But the dice do not move in the cheat's hand. The thrower holds the dice firmly in the bend of their middle and ring fingers, while the forefinger and little finger prevent them from rolling back and forth. The thumb prevents them from rotating on the other axis. The dice rattle against each other, as if their orientation is being randomized, producing the familiar sound known as a cackle so similar to the cackle of dice shaken fairly. The telltale signs that a thrower is cheating like this are the way they pick up the dice and the way the two inner knuckles protrude farther than the outer ones when the dice are in their hand. But rapid motion makes this latter telltale difficult to observe.

Holding the dice in the lock grip enables the cheat to rig the odds in their favor by means of throws that prevent certain num-bers from coming up. The whip shot (otherwise known as the pique shot, drop shot, or Hudson shot) is another technique that throws dice already set up in such a way that they land with the numbers the thrower intends. The dice are held in the lock grip with the wanted numbers facing upward. After the cackle of a false rattle, the dice are rolled by the thumb forward toward the fingertips. Then with a wrist movement like a whip, the dice are thrown. They spin without rotating along their horizontal axis and fall with the correct numbers facing upward. It is important that the dice do not bounce.

Another effective cheat is the blanket roll, which uses the lock grip to throw the dice on a soft playing surface, such as a blanket, carpet, bed, baize table, tablecloth, or soft earth. The dice are rolled from the lock-grip hand so that they rotate around only one axis, rolling like a wheel and then coming to rest. The blanket roll prevents the sides of each die facing the other and the outer opposite sides of the dice from turning up, thereby altering the odds.

As with the whip shot, the cheat first sets up the dice in the position to land as they want them to. Setting the dice means holding them in certain positions that will produce an advantageous score. One favored dice arrangement is the flying V, which involves holding the dice with the threes facing up, and the spots arranged in a *V* shape and using a controlled throw that prevents the inner and outer values from landing faceup, thereby reducing the chances of throwing a seven. It is interesting to note that the famous electric guitar, the Gibson Flying V, played by blues luminaries such as Albert King is named after this dice cheat roll.

An alternative means of rigging the outcome of a dice roll is the false throw. This involves shaking the dice in the hand and surreptitiously looking at the pips on the bottom of the dice before they are thrown. A seasoned dice player who has learned the full dice-setting technique with straight dice immediately knows the numbers of pips on the top of the dice, as opposite faces all add up to seven: one and six; two and five; four and three. If the numbers are those the dicer needs, then the false throw is made immediately. If not, they can imperceptibly move them with the thumb to the required numbers. Then the hand is slammed down with palm face down and the dice slide out to one side, rotating on their vertical axes with a spin but not rolling over. In a false throw, the required numbers remain on top.

Even when dice are thrown from a dice cup, preventing false throws with the hand, there are still ways to influence the outcome. In the false shake, the cheat puts the dice in the cup so that one is stacked squarely on top of the other, and they are standing against the side of the dice cup. The cup is held vertically and rotated in a circular motion that keeps the dice in the same relative position by centrifugal force. The dice then come out in the desired orientation, just as with a false throw. In dice games using more than two dice, such as buck dice and poker dice, a cheat is used that depends on holding one of the dice unseen against the rim of the cup, so that it is set down showing the desired value. This trick depends on sleight of hand. It gives a significant advantage to the cheat to have at least one die set up in this way.

Another more overt and potentially riskier way of cheating at dice is to use crooked dice that have been doctored in some way. Straight dice have a particular order of numbers one to six where opposite faces add up to seven, a convention that is essential for fair play, but of course dice need not be made that way. One way of cheating is to use misspotted (unconventionally spotted) dice known as busters, tees, tops, or horses. Most common are those that have the same number on opposing faces, which is not apparent because only three faces are visible at any one time. In games that need high numbers and doubles to win, cheats use misspotted high-number dice, a pair numbered with pips reading only four, five, and six.

There are various forms of busters used to cheat in conventional dice games, such as craps. The first die has faces numbered with only one, five, and six, and the second die is numbered with only three, four, and five. They can never score a two, three, seven, or twelve, the losing numbers in crap games. Other variants are high-low splitters, with one die numbered with one, two, and three and the other with four, five, and six, and dice called door pops are rigged to produce only a seven or eleven when thrown.

Dice that are perfectly formed, geometrically accurate, and equally balanced are known as straight dice, square dice, perfect dice, or level dice or are "on the square" and "on the level" (which is also a Masonic expression meaning a trusted person). Casinos use precision dice, which through meticulous manufacturing and precise quality control are made as accurate as possible. They have their pips drilled out and then filled with a special pigment that has the same specific gravity as the material used for the dice. This means that there is no imbalance whatsoever between sides with more or fewer pips. Of course, even perfect dice made to an engineering tolerance of one ten-thousandth of an inch still have imperfections. But at such a small level, the inaccuracies are negligible.

Crooked dice, on the other hand, have been doctored or fixed in some way that makes them fall in a nonrandom way that will skew the odds in favor of the user. "Rattling tatts" was a seventeenth-century English cant expression for crooked dice. In the eighteenth century they were called dispatches, and in the nineteenth century they were called charged dice. Nowadays they are usually called crooked or loaded dice.

There are a number of ways that dice can be fixed, gaffed, or loaded by an expert known as a dice gaffer or dice mechanic. Dice known as flats, shapes, or bricks may be made that are not truly cubic, since they have two sides that are square and four that are

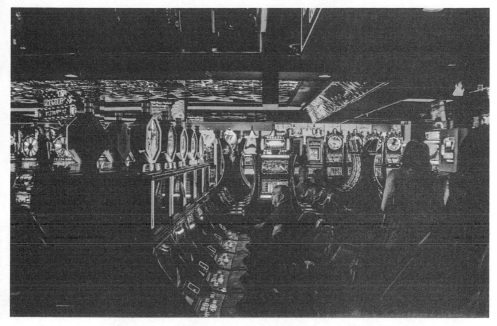

Fig. 5.2. In a casino on the Las Vegas Strip, 2017.
(Photograph by John Schnobrish)

shorter rectangles. Either of the two square sides will come up in most throws. Capped dice have one face made of a different, more elastic material than the other five. The die tends to bounce on this face, so the opposite face is less likely to turn up.

An early twentieth-century dice scam called the wire joint devised a fix using electric dice that had pieces of magnetic steel in the spots on four sides. The casino would call in a "juice man" to install an electromagnet unseen beneath the cloth on which the dice were thrown. It was provided with a button beneath the table or a foot-operated switch so that the cheating house could activate the magnet when needed. Electromagnets can be so powerful that they can turn over a static die when the power is switched on. The electric die lands with its unloaded sides top and bottom, as the magnetic field operates horizontally, thereby getting the dice to turn up the required numbers.

With dice that are geometrically cubic, slick dice are polished on one face and roughened on others to skew the odds. One of the oldest recorded kinds of fixed dice is the bristle, so-called because in former times dicers would insert a cut hog bristle or horsehair into the center of the five so that it would protrude slightly. This seventeenth-century bristle flipped the die off the unwanted number, whereas the current bristles have a protrusion that stops the die if it's rolled on a cloth surface.

Trip dice have flat faces as straight dice do, but some of the edges are roughened so that the dice will tend to fall statistically asymmetrically to the advantage of the dicer. Related to these are cut-edge dice and raised-edge dice. The cut-edge dice have one edge blunted at a 45 degree angle, and the other edges at 60 degree angles. Raised-edge dice have a lip on one edge that has more friction than the other sides when thrown on cloth, making it turn up more often than it statistically should. Conversely, round-edge or razor-edge dice have one edge shaved down, and sawtooth dice have one edge serrated to enable that edge to grip better and turn up the desired number.

Bevels are dice that are made not perfectly cubic, with one or more faces slightly convex so that there is a lower chance it will land with that side down. Dice may also have a concave side. These are called suction dice because it is believed that when thrown on a hard surface the indentation produces a lower air pressure, which tends to stop the die with the concave side lowermost. The indentation also favors rough surfaces, where it tends to finish rough side down. A fixed die may be hollowed out so that one side is lighter than the others, in which case it is called a floater, or it may have some dense material inserted into it near a corner or an edge that makes it heavier on one side, increasing the likelihood of it falling with the opposite side faceup. This is called a loaded or weighted die. Even transparent dice can be fixed by having the spots on one side contain a very dense material that skews the balance, making the die fall with the heavy side down and showing the opposite face, which is the desired number.

A type of crooked die that has been around for a very long time is the tapper, a die containing quicksilver, or the metal mercury, which is liquid at room temperatures. These dice have a hollow at the center containing a drop of quicksilver, and from this a capillary tube connects to another hollow on one side. The cheat loads the die before the throw by tapping it so the mercury flows from the center to the outer reservoir.

Related to the tapper is a more technical doctored die that has a similar principle but uses a chemical substance whose melting point is just a bit lower than human body heat. Warming the die in the hands causes the chemical to liquefy and flow to one side, like the mercury in the tapper, thereby producing the cheat's desired number.

Crooked dice players will also surreptitiously switch dice, using crooked dice for their throw and then switching back to straight dice.

None of this is new. Charles Cotton (1630–1687), in *The Compleat Gamester* published in 1674, described the crooked dice then in use in England:

This they do by false Dice, as High Fullams, 4, 5, 6. Low Fullams 1, 2, 3. By Bristle Dice, which are fitted for their purpose by sticking a Hog's bristle, so in the corners, or otherwise in the Dice, that they shall run high, or low, as they please. This bristle must be strong and short, by which means, the bristle bending, it will not lie on that side, but will be tript over; and this is the newest way of making a high, or low Fullam. The old ways are by drilling them, and loading them with quicksilver; but that cheat may be easily discovered by their weight, or holding two corners between your forefinger and thumb; if, holding them so, gently between your fingers, they turn, you may conclude them false: or, you may try their falsehood otherwise, by breaking, or splitting them. Others have made them by filing and rounding; but all these ways fall short of the Art of those who make them; some whereof are so admirably skilful in making a Bale of Dice to run what you would have them, that your Gamesters think they can never give enough for their purchase, if they prove right.

Ancient crooked dice have been found by archaeologists in a number of different cultures. It is assumed that these were used by gamblers to cheat. But they may well have been used at oracular shrines to skew the readings of those who came to ask questions. The different odds of different numbers turning up do not appear to have been present in the operation of ancient dice oracles, which are mathematically different from binary systems using cowrie

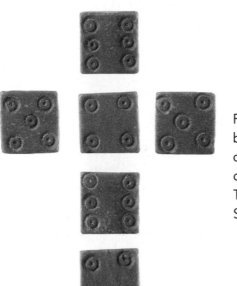

Fig. 5.3. A postmedieval bone cuboid false dice dating fifteenth–sixteenth century. (Courtesy of The Portable Antiquities Scheme)

Fig. 5.4. Man dicing with a skeleton, representing Death, 1767.
(Courtesy of the Wellcome Collection)

shells or other two-choice instruments. Although the concept of randomness had not yet been developed, it is naïve to imagine that priesthoods in antiquity were totally without any underhand practices. Contemporary priesthoods are not entirely without dishonest members, and there is no reason to have illusions that things were much different hundreds and thousands of years ago. Fortune tellers often tell their clients what they want to hear, and in times when priestesses and priests had to deal with ruthless tyrants and a wrong answer might mean torture and death of themselves, their families, and associates, it would have been prudent to hedge their bets and produce predictable results. When we dice with Death, we can be sure that Death has the dice in a special grip and throws all the shots, and the dice are probably loaded.

THE WAGER

·····································

*One Hundred Guineas
to One Penny*

WAGERS AND CONTEMPORARY
CHARITY WALKS

So long as they were not fixed by cheats, early systems of gambling depended on true randomness, as with dice or the dealing of cards. The emergence of the mathematics of probability led to gambling upon the outcome of sporting events, such as boxing and horse racing. There the bookmakers who ran the gambling offered odds upon the various fighters or horses, calculated according to earlier form. The odds were given as to the probability of one or another winning, and money was paid out to punters (bettors) according to their stake and the odds of the winner.

The technique of calculating the probability of a horse winning a race was extended to the probability of any event taking place, and wagers for and against the performance of feats of endurance then became a viable form of gambling. Wagers on walking and running were very popular in eighteenth-century Britain.

In 1793 Foster Powell, who, starting on November 29 of that year, wagered that he would walk from London to York and back in six days. He walked 88 miles from London to Stamford on the first day; the next day a farther 72 miles to Doncaster; on the third day 37 miles to York, and then 22 miles back to Ferrybridge. On the fourth day Powell walked 65 miles to Grantham, 54 miles to Eaton Socon on the fifth; and the final day saw him walk the final of 56 miles back to London, a total of 394 miles between Monday morning and Saturday night, winning the wager of one hundred guineas. In the early nineteenth century Captain Barclay wagered 5,000 guineas that he would walk 90 miles in 20 hours 30 minutes, which he succeeded in doing it in 19 hours 22 minutes.

In July 1809 Barclay wagered to walk a thousand miles in a thousand successive hours at the rate of a mile each and every hour. He had until four o'clock in the afternoon to finish this feat, but he performed his last mile in the quarter of an hour after three, "with perfect ease and great spirit, amidst an immense concourse of spectators." Captain Barclay won his £6,000 wager, and side bets were stated to amount to £100,000 (Ashton 1898, 168–169).

The current practice of walking, jogging, running, and swimming specified distances for charity derives directly from this earlier British wager tradition. It was given a massive boost in December 1959 when the vegetarian activist Dr. Barbara Moore (1903–1977) walked from Edinburgh to London. In 1960 she walked from John O'Groats to Land's End in twenty-three days and then carried out an even longer one from San Francisco to

New York in the same year. Her feat of vegetarian endurance was a media sensation. The wagers placed on participants in current charity events put the onus completely upon the punter.

Today, sponsorship has taken the place of the wager, and it is often paid even if the participant fails because it is seen as a charitable act. If the participant fails, the punter receives no financial gain as they would if it was a wager.

Although there are quite a few songs in American traditional folk music that mention dice playing, there are not as many from the English tradition until the ballads appeared. Among English folksongs collected around the turn of the twentieth century from village singers is one titled "The Penny Wager," or "Long Time I've Travelled in the North Country," which was collected from "a Hampshire man" by Geoffry Hill in Britford, Wiltshire, and published in *Wiltshire Folk Songs and Carols* in 1898. Hill collected it from an oral source, but archaized the spelling (e.g., "countrie"), making it appear quaint. I have revised it with standard spelling as follows:

> *Long time I've traveled in the North Country,*
> *A seeking for good company,*
> *Good company I always could find,*
> *But none that suited to my mind.*
> *To sing wack fal the ral,*
> *Ral the riddle dee,*
> *I've in my pocket but one penny.*
> *Oh there I saw three noble knights,*
> *As they were a playing of dice,*
> *As they were at play and I looked on,*
> *They took me to be some noble man.*
> *To sing wack fal the ral,*
> *Ral the riddle dee,*

I've in my pocket but one penny.
They asked me if I would play,
I asked they what bets they would lay,
The one says a guinea, the other five pound,
The bet it was made, put the money down.
To sing wack fal the ral,
Ral the riddle dee,
I've in my pocket but one penny.
I took up the dice and threw them in,
'Twas my good fortune to win.
If they had o' won and I had o' lost,
I must have shook out my empty purse.
And sung wack fal the ral,
Ral the riddle dee,
I've in my pocket but one penny.
Was there ever a mortal man so glad,
As I was with the money I had?
I'm a hearty good fellow and that you shall find,
I'll make you all drunk boys a drinking of wine.
To sing wack fal the ral,
Ral the riddle dee,
I've in my pocket but one penny.
I tarried all night and part the next day,
Till I thought it high time to be jogging away.
I asked the young landlady what was to pay,
Oh, only one kiss my love, go your way.
And sing wack fal the ral,
Ral the riddle dee,
I've in my pocket but one penny.

Another version of this song, titled "No Money and Plenty," was "obtained of James Mills, South Cerney," by Alfred Williams and published in *The Wilts and Gloucestershire Standard*, November 27, 1915. Williams stated, "I have also heard it spoken of at Bradon. The style discovers its age; it is of eighteenth-century date, or earlier." Following Geoffry Hill, Williams also archaized the spelling (such as with "countree"). Here standard spelling is again used:

> *I often traveled the North Country,*
> *Seeking for good company;*
> *Good company I could always find,*
> *But never one girl to my mind.*
> *Whack fol i dee,*
> *Whack fol i dee,*
> *And in my pocket not one penny.*
> *I saddled my pony and away I did ride,*
> *Till I came to an alehouse close by the roadside;*
> *I boldly got off and I sat myself down,*
> *And called for a jug of good ale that was brown.*
> *Whack fol i dee,*
> *Whack fol i dee,*
> *And in my pocket not one penny.*
> *As I sat drinking in front of my eyes,*
> *There were two gentlemen playing at dice;*
> *As they were at play, and I looking on,*
> *They took me to be a respectable man.*
> *Whack fol i dee,*
> *Whack fol i dee,*
> *And in my pocket not one penny.*
> *As I sat there, they asked me to play,*
> *I asked them the wager, what would they lay;*
> *One said a guinea, the other five pound,*
> *The wager was laid, but the money not down.*

Whack fol i dee,
Whack fol i dee,
And in my pocket not one penny.
I picked up the dice, I threw them all in,
It happened to be my good fortune to win;
If they had won, and I should have lost,
Then I must have sold my little black horse.
Whack fol i dee,
Whack fol i dee,
And in my pocket not one penny.
I stopped there all night, until the next day,
I asked the landlady what I had to pay;
She said, "Kiss me and love me, and then go your
     way,
If you stop any longer you'll have money to pay."
Whack fol i dee,
Whack fol i dee,
And in my pocket not one penny.

The actual dice game played in the song is not named. As most gambling games involve raising the stakes, the first version is an unlikely scenario, and his horse in the second is a more likely stake than a penny. Songs about people at the lower end of the class system getting advantage over their "betters" have always been popular.

By contrast, an American blues song that takes dice playing as its key theme refers to elements of the game of craps and the loss that gambling brings. "Crapshooter's Blues" was written by the American bluesman Peetie Wheatstraw (given name William Bunch, 1902–1941), whose hoodoo-man credentials gave him the epithets the High Sheriff from Hell and the Devil's Son-in-Law. Wheatstraw was a guitarist and piano player in St. Louis,

Missouri. Befitting his magical status, he was born on the winter solstice in 1902 and died in a car crash with a train on a level crossing on his thirty-ninth birthday on the winter solstice, 1941, highly symbolically perishing at a crossroads, albeit road and railroad. Some of his songs contained policy numbers, which will be explained in the next chapter. Wheatstraw's "Crapshooter's Blues" is a classic of its kind.

GAMBLING
AND GAMING

·····································

The Prohibition
of Practices Pre-1880

As a place for gambling, the Stock Exchange is of far greater extent than the Turf. The time bargains and options, without which the business of the Exchange would be very little, are gambling pure and simple, while the numerous bucket shops, with their advertisements and circulars, disseminate the unwholesome vice of gambling throughout the length and breadth of the land, enabling people to speculate without anyone being the wiser. It is needless to say, that, as on the Turf, they are the losers.

JOHN ASHTON,
THE HISTORY OF GAMBLING IN ENGLAND

*T*hose in authority have always been the kind of people John Michell called "world improvers," using their power to ban all sorts of practices they consider harmful. If only certain customs and practices were banned, the argument goes, the world would be a better place and more nearly approximate to the paradise that the world improvers aspire to. The ban on smoking in public places is the most recent of these bans, which have a long history. In 1928, cannabis was banned in the United Kingdom for the same reason, and drug and alcohol bans in other lands have similarly failed to prevent the commodities being traded and used and instead have produced a steep rise in organized crime. In former times, these bans were carried out as religious edicts; today, a utilitarian argument is used.

In the West, the religious objections to gambling originate in antiquity in the Jewish religion. In Biblical times, among the Jews money won by gaming was viewed as having been obtained by theft. It was a punishable offense under religious law but only when the gaming had been among Jews. It was not unlawful to win money when gambling with a Gentile. However, gambling in principle, whether with fellow Jew or Gentile, was condemned for another reason. According to the Talmudists,

> it does not become a man, at any time of his life, to make anything his business which does not relate to the study of wisdom or the public good . . . this was only a prohibition of their doctors, perhaps the law, or usage in such cases might take place, that the offender was to be scourged. (Ashton 1898, 6)

Gambling with dice is known from the medieval period from those who condemned it as foolish or evil. It was not only dice that were banned but virtually all game playing, as extreme

religious laws were the order of the day. Ordericus Vitalis
(1075–1143) wrote, "the clergymen and bishops are fond of dice-
playing" and John of Salisbury (1110–1182) called it "the dam-
nable art of dice-playing." John Ashton wrote,

> In 1190 a curious edict was promulgated, which shows how
> generally gambling prevailed even among the lower classes at
> that period. This edict was established for the regulation of
> the Christian army under the command of Richard the First
> of England and Philip of France during the Crusade. It pro-
> hibits any person in the army, beneath the degree of knight,
> from playing at any sort of game for money; knights and cler-
> gymen might play for money, but none of them were permit-
> ted to lose more than twenty shillings in one whole day and
> night, under a penalty of one hundred shillings, to be paid to
> the archbishops in the army. The two monarchs had the privi-
> lege of playing for what they pleased, but their attendants were
> restricted to the sum of twenty shillings, and, if they exceeded,
> they were to be whipped naked through the army for three
> days. The decrees established by the Council held at Worcester
> in the twenty-fourth year of Henry III prohibited the clergy
> from playing at dice or chess, but neither the one nor the other
> of these games are mentioned in the succeeding statutes before
> the twelfth year of Richard II., when dicing is particularised
> and expressly forbidden. (Ashton 1898, 13)

It was not only among the Anglo-Norman monarchs that dicing was forbidden. *Gragas,* the ancient law code of north Norway,
forbade dicing and condemned those caught playing dice to be
declared outlaw. When the independent republic of Iceland was
annexed by Norway, King Magnus Haakonsson (1263–1280)
enacted a law against dice playing (Fiske 1905, 331). In London in

1334, under King Edward III, a proclamation banned mumming and dice playing:

> Also, we do forbid, on the same pain of imprisonment, that any man shall go about, at this Feast of Christmas, with companions disguised with false faces [masks], or in any other manner, to the houses of the good folks of the City, for playing at dice there; but let each one keep himself quiet and at his ease within his own house. (Ashton 1898, 15–16)

But while it is easy to make a proclamation or pass a new law, it is a lot more difficult to enforce it, especially when the purpose of the law is to suppress a popular pastime that the people view as harmless. So dicing went on, as popular as ever, despite repeated legal pronouncements against it. William Shakespeare mentions dice and dicing thirteen times in seven of his plays, and other dramatists of his era make many allusions to it.

Although it was illegal, and there are some notable recorded cases of severe punishment for professional dicers who cheated others, it is clear that prosecutions for gambling with dice were relatively rare in medieval England. For example, of 1,659 recorded cases tried in the Norwich leet courts between 1288 and 1391, only one charge of dicing was brought (Maddern 2004, 196). But nevertheless the prohibition of games was an obsession. Christmas was deemed to be the only time that games were allowed, and playing at other times was forbidden by law. The connection of gambling with misrule is overt in writings about carnivals and mythical lands, such as the Land of Cokaygne. *Carmina Burana* contains a song that dates from around 1164 in which the Abbas Cucaniensis encourages his brothers to drink and play dice:

I am the Abbot of Cokaygne,
And I take counsel with my drinking companions
And my part is of the fraternity of gamblers,
And if anyone asks me in the tavern at Matins
Come Vespers, I will have the shirt off his back;
And so being fleeced of his clothes he will cry:
'Save me! Save me! What have you done, you
    god-forsaken dice?
Now you've made me sacrifice
All I knew of Paradise'

This title, Abbas Cucaniensis, the Abbot of Cokaygne, is another title of the Abbot of Unreason or Lord of Misrule who traditionally oversees the festivities of yule and carnival.

Religiously, gambling was viewed as transgressive, and Ashton writes,

> legislation about cards was thought necessary in Henry VIII's time, for we see in 33 Hen. VIII, cap. 9, sec. xvi: "Be it also enacted by the authority aforesaid. That no manner of artificer, or craftsman of any handicraft or occupation, husbandman, apprentice, labourer, servant at husbandry, journeyman, or servant of artificer, mariners, fishermen, watermen, or any serving man, shall from the said feast of the Nativity of St. John Baptist, play at the tables, tennis, dice, cards, bowls, clash, coyting, legating, or any unlawful game, out of Christmas, under the pain of 20 shillings to be forfeit for every time. (Ashton 1898, 40)

But it was not only dice that got people into trouble with the law. In the second half of the sixteenth century, after the passing of the repressive laws against all sports and games except archery by King Henry VIII in 1533, people in England were prosecuted for playing "unlawful games" such as cards, bowls, alleys (marbles), skittles, slidethrift, and shove-groat (later known as shove ha'penny). As F. G. Emmison noted, "nearly all Englishmen were prohibited from playing nearly all games" (Emmison 1970). The persecution of games, which of course included dice, continued until after the English Civil War and Cromwell's republic, when, with the restoration of King Charles II in 1660, the laws were effectively discontinued.

Before all forms of gambling were legalized in the United Kingdom in the second half of the twentieth century, the late seventeenth and eighteenth centuries were seen as the heyday of British gambling. For example, the comedy *The Gamester* (1705) by Susanna Centlivre (c. 1667–1723) has an epilogue addressed to the audience:

> *You Roaring Boys, who know the Midnight Cares*
> *Of Rattling Tatts, ye Sons of Hopes and Fears;*
> *Who Labour hard to bring your Ruin on,*
> *And diligently toil to be undone;*
> *You're Fortune's sporting Footballs at the best,*
> *Few are his Joys, and small the Gamester's Rest:*
> *Suppose then, Fortune only rules the Dice,*
> *And on the Square you Play; yet, who that's Wise*
> *Wou'd to the Credit of a Faithless Main*
> *Trust his good Dad's hard-gotten hoarded Gain?*
> *But, then, such Vultures round a Table wait,*
> *And, hovering, watch the Bubble's sickly State;*
> *The young fond Gambler, covetous of more,*
> *Like Esofis Dog, loses his certain Store.*
> *Then the Spring squeez'd by all, grows dry, And,*
> *   now,*

Compleatly Wretched, turns a Sharper too;
These Fools, for want of Bubbles, too, play Fair,
And lose to one another on the Square.
This Itch for Play, has, likewise, fatal been,
And more than Cupid drawn the Ladies in,
A Thousand Guineas for Basset prevails,
A Bait when Cash runs low, that seldom fails;
And, when the Fair One can't the Debt defray,
In Sterling Coin, does Sterling Beauty pay.

An illegal gambling racket popular in early twentieth-century England was pitch and toss. This involved betting on the outcome of three coins being placed on the ends of two fingers and tossed in the air to land on the ground: three heads, three tails; a head and two tails; or a tail and two heads. The simple equipment required for this game, ordinary coins, were not incriminating gambling artefacts like dice, cards, or the pea and the walnut shells.

In Sheffield in the 1910s and 1920s, notoriously violent gangsters ran the pitch and toss racket at pitches located at Sky Edge (on a hilltop called Skyring), Wadsley, Five Arches, and Tinsley. The business was called a joint and the ring, a pitch. The head of the racket was a man called the toller, who collected the tolls on the bets, a certain percentage of each bet, which went to the business (called in some forms of gambling the service charge or vigorish). Around the toller were his strong-arm associates who worked under a man called the ponter, who was armed with a stick. Further out were other gang members, called pilners, who were scouts who kept an eye on goings-on and also watched out for the police.

The bets were placed in the ring, and then the tosser threw the three halfpennies. Winnings were paid out by the toller, new bets were placed, and another toss took place. As in craps and other dice games, there were also side bets placed between individual punters (gamesters). Police attempts to suppress this form of gambling involved mass arrests of participants, but only with the suppression of the gangs after a series of brutal murders, did this form of gambling fade out (Bean 1981, 7–8).

It is a notable phenomenon that almost every time a new law is introduced to regulate or suppress something, it immediately has unintended consequences that may even create problems worse than the problems that it is intended to prevent. In 1853 the British Parliament made it illegal to bet on horseracing with cash at any place except at the racecourse (racetrack). Bets could be telegraphed or later telephoned to a commission agent's office, but betting was strictly illegal.

This law, of course, led to a thriving trade in street bookmaking, the equivalent of the numbers racket in America (see chapter 8). Illegal street bookmakers were a common sight in British cities and towns until the legalization of betting shops in the 1960s. Street bookmakers employed touts, who kept watch for the police, and runners, who collected bets from anywhere anyone wanted to gamble: shop, factory, works, mill, mine, station, depot, and dock. Far from suppressing gambling, the law created an underworld structure of organized crime that promoted it.

And indeed, it appears that even the lawyers ignored the laws against gambling, for when the floors of the Middle Temple Hall in London were taken up in the 1760s, among other things were found nearly a hundred pairs of dice that had fallen through the chinks of the flooring. People are resourceful and will always find ingenious ways to get around repressive laws. When one particular form of gambling was invented, eventually it was banned along with all the other, older forms. By then, a new means had been found that was not illegal, and it went into use until it, too, came to the notice of the authorities and was banned. The contemporary parallels to this are designer drugs, or legal highs, which are legal until banned, at which time another new one will be created to take its place. The evolution of gambling techniques and designer drugs is a social example of Darwin's natural selection.

In London in 1808, J. P. Malcolm noted,

> however unpleasant the yells of barrow women with their commodities are at present, no other mischief arises from them than the obstruction of the ways. It was far otherwise before 1716 when they generally carried Dice with them, and children were enticed to throw for fruit and nuts, or, indeed, any persons of a more advanced age. However, in the year just mentioned, the Lord Mayor issued an order to apprehend all retailers so offending, which speedily put an end to street gaming; though I am sorry to observe that some miscreants now (1808)

Fig. 7.1. Wheel of Fortune, Rotterdam c. 1800. (Nigel Pennick Collection)

HET RAD VAN AVONTUUR.

carry little wheels marked with numbers, which, being turned, govern the chance by the figure a hand in the centre points to when stopped. (Malcolm quoted by Ashton, 1898, 28)

In 1898, John Ashton wrote of this phenomenon:

When I was young the itinerant vendors of sweets had a "dolly," which was a rude representation of a man, hollowed spirally; a marble was dropped in at its head, and coming out at its toes, spun round a board until it finally subsided into one of the numerous numbered hollows it contained. When that was made illegal, a numbered teetotum was used, and now childhood is beguiled with the promise of a threepenny piece, or other prize, to be found in packets of sweets. (Ashton 1898, 28)

ILLEGAL GAMBLING'S INTERSECTION WITH DIVINATION AND MAGIC

1880s to the Present

he original prohibitions on divination that originated in ancient Jewish scriptures were enacted not because the practice was deemed meaningless and futile, but because it was believed in and feared. The fear was twofold: firstly, divination was believed to work because it enabled the diviner to gain access to evil spirits that produced a view of what was to come. This was deemed illegitimate by the priests who had appropriated all powers of supernatural contact for their own exclusive use. The second fear was that God, having his plans revealed in advance by divination, would, like the local Bronze Age warlords on which he was modeled, punish his subjects for their presumption.

This fatalistic worldview stifled curiosity and experiment,

and it was outside the Jewish religion that divination developed. Perhaps the ancient Jewish prohibition of divination, which was taken up wholesale and unthinkingly into the Christian religion when Christianity split off from Judaism, accelerated the desacralization of divination into gambling. Techniques that had been used to determine the will of the gods, or events yet to come, were used as exciting secular games in which money could change hands. Secularization of sacred rites is a theme throughout history; the desacralization of alcohol drinking and smoking tobacco, both once sacred rituals, are two notable examples. Although most divination systems are based on random results, and the outcome of fair gambling using numbers is also random, the use of divination to determine the winning numbers in lotteries has been and is widespread. The two means are never far apart.

In the United States, racketeers ran the numbers game, otherwise known as bolita or policy. It was an illegal lottery said to have originated in Chicago in 1885. The founder of this lottery was a gangster known only as Policy Sam. It spread rapidly across the country, and it was banned in 1901. But being made illegal did not close it down. The racket was operated through street "numbers runners," the American equivalent of the street bookmakers' agents, who were a common sight in Great Britain at that period, conducting illegal street betting on horse racing.

Like the British street bookies, numbers runners, who were also operating their illegal gambling racket openly, had recognized codes of behavior. The name policy came from the question runners asked: "Would you like to take out an insurance policy?" There were also policy shops and policy offices, where front businesses like barbershops or tobacconists would cover for the real business of the illegal lottery. By the time it had become endemic in the United States, various "companies" (gangs) were operating the numbers game. They were called such names as the East and

West, the Interstate, the Streamliner, and the Red Devil. These names also referred to the actual lottery wheels on which the numbers were generated. The wheels were spun several times a day, the numbers "fell," and winnings were paid out.

Thomas Knox, a New York journalist, published an account of the policy game in 1892, when it was spreading across the United States:

> "Playing policy" is a cheap way of gambling, but one on which hundreds if not thousands of dollars are risked every day in New York. Sums as low as three cents can be risked upon it, and there are policy-shops where bets of one cent are taken. The play is upon numbers which are drawn daily, usually in Kentucky or Louisiana, and sent by telegraph. The numbers are from 1 to 78; the room where the game is played is, like those of other cheap gambling-dens, usually at the rear of a cigar-store, barroom or other place where it does not rouse suspicion if many persons are seen entering. A long counter extends the entire length of the room, and behind this counter, near its center sits the man who keeps the game and is called the "writer." He is not the proprietor, but simply a clerk on a salary, and his duties are to copy the slips handed up by the players, mark them with the amount of money paid, and watch to see that no fraud is practiced.
>
> There are twenty-five plays every morning and the same number in the evening at the regular shops, and they all get their winning numbers from a central office in Broad Street. Near the "writer" is an iron spike or hook on which are the policy slips; each slip contains the winning numbers and is placed faced downwards so that nobody can see what it is. Let us now see how the scheme is worked. I am about to try my luck at policy, and for this purpose enter a shop and pass

through to the rear. . . . Along the counter are numerous slips of paper for general use. I take one of the slips and write upon it five pairs of numbers [he means trios of numbers, not pairs, as will be seen], using any numbers from 1 to 78. I give this slip to the "writer," with fifteen cents, and say, "Put me in for five gigs at three cents."

Two numbers are called a "saddle" and three numbers a "gig." There are numerous combinations in the game, but "gigs" and "saddles" are the most popular. I wait until the other players have put in their bets, which the "writer" copies and records and then hands back to the players, just as he copies and returns mine. When all the bets are in, he takes the first policy slip from the spike or hook aforesaid, writes upon a slate the numbers he finds on the slip and then hangs it up where everybody can see it. He writes them in two columns of twelve numbers, and if I have guessed two of the numbers in either column in one of my gigs, I walk up to the counter and present my ticket for payment, receiving ten times the amount of my wager. But a man stands as good a chance of being struck by lightning as he does of winning at this rate. Nevertheless the game is full of seductiveness on account of its possibilities and also on account of its cheapness. Some of the shops have telephone connections, and a customer who is known to the establishment can play policy without leaving his office by simply telephoning his guesses. (Campbell, Knox, and Byrnes 1892, 639–40)

The gambling system of the numbers game was based on selecting groups of numbers between 1 and 78, the number of cards in a tarot pack. Although it was a lottery based on the wheel of fortune principle, much of its terminology came from horse racing. So a two-number bet was a "saddle," a three-number bet was a "gig," and a four-number bet was a "horse." The largest number combination allowed was twenty-five.

Popular gigs had specific names, and these number groups became a kind of meaningful code that appeared in popular songs from the 1920s onward, especially in the blues of the 1920s to the 1940s. For example, the Dirty Gig was three, six, and nine, and it appeared in the New Orleans song "Iko Iko." The Washerwoman's Gig was four, eleven, forty-four. It appears in the hit song "4.11.44" by banjo player Papa Charlie Jackson, issued in 1926, with the refrain "always keep playing four, eleven, forty-four." Among others, Peetie Wheatstraw, Blind Blake, and Kokomo Arnold employed policy number imagery in their blues songs, as certain numbers were a form of coded message. "Policy Blues" by Blind Blake (1930) tells how numbers are about to drive him mad, for he played three, six, nine and lost his money. But the numbers actually have a sexual connotation. He begs his woman to let him through her door, as he wants to put his twenty-five, fifty, seventy-five in her seven, seventeen, twenty-four and will continue playing fifteen, fifty, fifty-one until he has good luck.

The racket proved most attractive to African American gamblers—hence its appearance in blues songs—and it is for that ethnic group that a lucrative business of divinatory and magical books and accessories developed. In 1889, *Aunt Sally's Policy Players Dream Book* was published by Henry J. Wehman. In it are nine lists of motifs and objects that may appear in dreams that are connected by Aunt Sally to lucky numbers that may win at policy. This book contains *Napoleon's Oraculum* or *Book of Fate,* a text on divinatory geomancy. As with nongambling, oriented dream books, the dream motifs are arranged in alphabetical order. Each motif is accompanied by one, two, three, or four numbers that the dream indicates should be the winning numbers.

Aunt Sally's book has undergone many reprints and is still

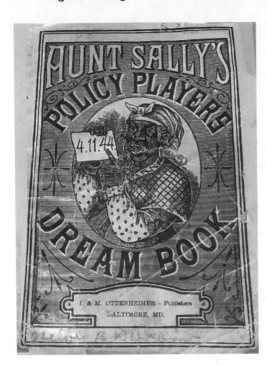

Fig. 8.1. The cover of *Aunt Sally's Policy Players Dream Book,* 1889.

available. In the 1940s, the King Novelty Company, among other things a supplier of hoodoo materia magica sold, along with *Aunt Sally's Policy Players Dream Book,* Aunt Sally's incense and potions, supposedly so the user could gamble and win. "Aunt Sally" in England refers to a throwing game related to skittles or ninepins, played at pubs or as a fairground sideshow. Among the "sticks," or skittles, is a larger figure, the "doll," which is placed upon an iron rod. This "doll" is Aunt Sally. By the 1970s, the game had dwindled and was more or less confined to Oxfordshire (Finn 1975, 79–84), but the name Aunt Sally is still used to describe something that has been set up as a target for abuse.

The title *Dream Book* actually became a code for a book of lucky numbers for policy, and various rival versions were published over the years. Few were as overt as the *Pick 'Em Dream Book* of Raja Rabo, and at least one was written by a hoodoo practitioner.

The image of lucky Aunt Sally was appropriated in 1967 by

San Francisco psychedelic artist Rick Griffin and used on a poster advertising *A Magic Show* starring the blues-orientated bands Big Brother and the Holding Company and the Canned Heat Blues Band. Instead of pointing to a card with "4-11-44" upon it, as on the *Dream Book* cover, Aunt Sally indicates the venue: the Avalon Ballroom (McClelland 1980, 15).

Benjamin Rucker (1892–1934), who performed stage magic as Black Herman, and published *Secrets of Magic, Mystery and Legerdemain* in 1925, also marketing incense under a Black Herman label to burn for success in the numbers game or other gambling. Black Herman was a practicing root doctor as well as a performing stage magician. Root doctors developed "lucky dream incense" that was burned by gamblers in their bedrooms before going to sleep, supposedly to promote prophetic dreams of the numbers that would fall in the policy games the next day. Some varieties of incense were made with small incombustible three-digit numbers in them that could be found in the ash the next day and used in the lottery.

SUPERSTITION IN THE GAMBLING LIFE

The Black Cat Plays an Ace of Spades

MAGIC INFLUENCES THE OUTCOME

The concepts of randomness and probability have no place in traditional magic, where the operants seek by esoteric means to influence the outcome of a particular event. The Northern Tradition worldview sees luck as a personal possession; there are instances from former times that interpret luck in this way. Luck is very complex; there are no direct quotes in Norse sagas, but themes are embedded within them. The Viga-Glúms Saga demonstrates how luck is understood as an aspect of one's personality and lineage. As a personal possession, luck must be nurtured, for it can also be lost. The old Irish adage "There is no money that cannot be stolen" applies also to luck. Those who trust in divination employ esoteric means to *predict* the outcome of an event that otherwise is uninfluenced; magicians, on the other hand, seek to *produce* their desired outcome. Lucky charms, mascots, amulets, and talismans are all magical means used by gamblers to improve their luck.

There are three kinds of magic used in gambling. The first seeks to solely influence the outcome of the game to the magician's advantage. The second seeks to disempower one's opponents' luck so that they lose. The third is counter magic, which involves using warding and blocking techniques against other magic that one's opponents might be using. Some types of magic are more common in one place than another and so fall into the flawed concept of regional or national magic. Available materia magica naturally varies from place to place—it always has. The materials used in Great Britain and Ireland vary only a little from the talismans, amulets, mascots, and lucky charms used in mainland Europe and Scandinavia and somewhat more than those classified as belonging to American hoodoo, conjure, and rootwork.

Magical techniques are not nationalistic. Whatever is deemed to work will be adopted, wherever the magician lives. If there is a material in America that is known to have a specific function, and there is no equivalent in Europe that serves an identical purpose, the American material will be obtained. John the Conqueror root, for instance, one of the most famous power materials in hoodoo, used to draw money and love, is not indigenous to Europe but can be obtained there, as can the penis bone of the raccoon and the five-finger grass herb used in American gambling magic.

In America, the techniques written in European magical books, such as the revered *Romanus-Büchlein*, were integrated with magical techniques of Native American and African origins to create the present-day magical systems called powwowing, hoodoo, conjure, and rootwork. Similarly, in the West Indies, the African divination and magic practiced by some slaves was melded with magical techniques from the Indigenous Caribs, from Europe and the Indian subcontinent, to make the system known as Obeah (Pennick 2011, 125–130).

OMENS, OSTENTA, AND SUPERSTITION

As with many trades, there are omens that one must take notice of when gambling, and things that must or must not be done. For example, the old quarrymen of Portland in Dorset, England, would return home for the day if they saw a hare on their walk to the quarry, fishermen were loath to put to sea on Fridays, and many footballers (soccer players) today always put either the left or right shoe on first.

Luck-bringing magic is a significant element of gambling culture. Because luck is a tenuous and changeable thing, the circumstances surrounding gambling must be correct if the gambler is to get the best outcome.

Entering a place where one is to gamble through the main door is considered by some to be unlucky. Black is an unlucky color, so one should not wear black when gambling, as it will bring loss. This applies even when gambling online. Dogs are generally considered unlucky if they are near the dice or other gambling games. One can be "dogged" by bad luck, or the hellhound can be on one's trail, so dogs must not be allowed near the game.

One general superstition that naturally applies also to gambling is that of the broken mirror, which is said to bring seven years' worth of bad luck. And while few gamblers would give up gambling for years on that account, if a mirror at home should crack or be shattered accidentally, any plans to gamble that day must be canceled.

When gambling, if two gamblers accidentally touch shoulders, this will bring bad luck to both of them. If, during a game, a gambler should count their money, bad luck will follow, for this is tempting fate and the punter will soon have less or none at all to count.

Some gamblers' magic or superstitions verge on obsessive-compulsive disorder. Some insist on repeatedly washing their hands in magical oils or with special lucky soaps containing significant ingredients such as chamomile. Some dice players blow on the dice before throwing them, though this is suspect because of the old practice of using moisture- or heat-activated sticky

Fig. 9.1. "Rosary" of dice that can be used for divination or as a lucky gambling charm. (Nigel Pennick Collection)

materials to make dice adhere to enable crooked throws. Another obsession is orderliness: some gamblers insist that their gambling chips must be stacked precisely, or bad luck will ensue.

THE DEVIL'S IN THE CARDS

Certain cards have meanings outside those given to them by practitioners of cartomancy. It is not part of the remit of this book to discuss the cartomantic meanings of individual cards, whether of the playing card or tarot variety. But within gambling and more general lore, like geomantic figures and dice scores, certain cards are considered special or dangerous.

The ace of spades is perhaps the most famous or notorious card in the whole pack, often associated with death and the Devil. Some cartomancers take the ace of spades to actually signify death, though the queen of spades also appears in this context in American tradition. Arguably the most famous song of the heavy metal band Motörhead was "Ace of Spades," with the imagery of fast living and danger. The ace of spades even appears on a church, as George Tyack noted in 1899: "The tower of Ashton-under-Lyne had several yards of its masonry built by a woman, who suddenly appeared among the workmen, and found them engaged in playing cards. She promised to do a portion of their labour for them if they succeeded in turning up an ace; and, luckily for them, the next card in the pack proved to be the ace of spades. In memory of this strange occurrence an ace of spades was carved upon the tower" (Tyack 1899, 45).

Being dealt a long sequence of black cards is considered unlucky. It was formerly held to be prophetic of the death of the player or a family member. An Irish adage warns us to always look at a man's foot before you play cards with him, and don't play if he has a cloven foot, for he is the Devil. Another story tells of how men playing cards on a Saturday night suddenly noticed at midnight there was another player in their midst. Sunday had arrived, and the extra player was the Devil (Roud 2003, 62). The association of cards with the Devil is likely to be a cultural leftover from the centuries of religious fulmination against games and the religiously motivated laws that prohibited all forms of play and gambling for so many centuries.

The four of clubs was another card associated with the Devil and thus considered bad. In 1879 a Worcestershire farmer was quoted as saying, "There never was a good hand at cards if the four of clubs was in it . . . because the four of clubs in an unlucky card; it's the Devil's own card . . . the Devil's four-post bedstead" (*Notes & Queries* 5th series, Volume 12, 426). In Scottish card-playing tradition, the nine of diamonds is called the "Curse of Scotland." In her *Signs and Superstitions* (c. 1900), Helen Greig Souter noted three possible plausible explanations. One is the card game of comette, or colimette, which was introduced to Scotland by Mary Queen of Scots and became such a gambling addiction that it led to the financial ruin of many noble families. The winning card of comette is the nine of diamonds. Another origin of the "Curse of Scotland" is the clan and sectarian hatred of John Dalrymple, the first Earl of Stair, for his involvement in the massacre of Glencoe. John Dalrymple's coat of arms was a saltire bearing nine lozenges, seen popularly as the nine of diamonds. Finally, Souter tells us, the word *curse* is thought to be a corruption of the word *cross,* and the nine diamonds on the card were traditionally arranged to form a St. Andrew's Cross, the saltire of Scotland.

LUCKY CHARMS

In addition to these superstitions, there are many amulets, lucky charms, mascots, and talismans that gamblers use in their quest to get an edge over the game. In certain contexts, dice are themselves lucky charms; for example, a pair of dice showing the lucky number seven that may be actual dice, fuzzy dice hung in a car, or dice made of precious metal worn on a charm bracelet.

Although it is infrequently used, the term *mascot* means a bringer of good luck and is used to include amulets, charms, and talismans. These include "lucky" items of clothing or jewelry, items dyed a specific color, rabbits' feet, four-leafed clovers, and lucky bodily postures such as crossed fingers. In her work on these luck bringers, *The Mascot Book,* Elizabeth Villiers noted,

> the airman carries his luck bringer in his "bus" when he attempts his greatest flights; the motorist has a mascot on his car. Tennis players, even the most celebrated champions, go to the court thus protected, so boxers enter the ring. Cricketers and footballers go to the ground with their mascots, while the thousands of spectators who watch the matches carry the chosen luck-bringers of their favorites, hoping to give them victory. In racing it is the same, and it is well known that of all men gamblers have the greatest belief in luck bringers. May it not be suggested that the reason is because they study the subject more deeply than most people? (Villiers 1923, 9)

And as an example of a specific gambling mascots, Villiers wrote, "Badger. One of the animal's teeth is a gambler's mascot. This should be sewn in the right-hand pocket of the waistcoat to ensure good fortune when playing cards" (Villiers 1923, 21).

Other popular gambling mascots include a lucky coin bearing the year date of the gambler's birth and, in the American hoodoo tradition, carrying a mojo hand or conjure bag containing appropriate objects and materia magica prepared according to rituals intended to empower the gambler.

Many contemporary American sports teams and British football clubs have a living mascot, often a person dressed in an animal suit related to the team's or club's iconography (e.g., a dolphin for the Miami Dolphins football team and a swan for Swansea City soccer club, and a wolf for Wolverhampton Wanderers football club), who comes on the pitch (field) before the game starts, supposedly to bring the team good luck.

Villiers' theory on "how mascots gain their power" was as follows:

Originally the word 'influence' was used astrologically and referred only to the occult power, the virtue, that was believed to flow from the planets to affect all things on earth. Thus the word is used in its strictest sense if we say that mascots have no power of their own, but serve to attract the influence of the Unknown and thus they benefit mankind. (Villiers 1923, 6)

Villiers also believed that no mascot will bring good fortune to one who is unworthy of it.

The skull is a mascot often used by gamblers and others who flirt with danger, such as motorcyclists. The Prussian army had the Death's Head Hussars who wore on their heads a busby with a large metal representation of a human skull upon it. It had the function of terrifying the Hussars' opponents, telling them that no quarter would be given, that they would not be taken prisoner, but would be killed. In the United Kingdom, the equivalent cavalry unit was the lancers whose badge was similarly a skull and a ribbon with "or glory" written upon it, their motto being "Death or Glory." In the 1930s the German National Socialists appropriated the Prussian hussars' skull as a cap badge of the élite military corps known as the SS, and after World War II, with the widespread availability of German militaria taken as booty from dead or defeated soldiers, it was adopted by motorcyclists.

As the infamous Jolly Roger, the skull appeared on the flags of seventeenth- and eighteenth-century pirates, an addition to the black flag, which customarily declared "no quarter" in European military practice. Like the Death's Head Hussars' skull, the black flag meant that no prisoners would be taken, and everyone on the losing side would be killed. It was adopted as an anarchist emblem in 1832 (*The Symbol* Volume 1, 1983, 12), and appears today as the black flag of Islamic jihad.

In 1982, the British nuclear submarine *Conqueror* flew the Jolly Roger after having sunk the Argentine cruiser *General Belgrano* with huge loss of life in the Falklands War. As a symbol of violent theft on a large scale, and the famous buccaneering tales of the fabulous treasure the pirates accumulated, the Jolly Roger is another link between the skull and money, the gaining of which is the object of gambling.

Hoodoo expert Catherine Yronwode notes that the skull mascot used by American hard-core gamblers as a lucky charm is an instance of "reverse bad luck," signifying luck in adversity. Skull images on stickpins or watch fobs were also worn by gamblers. The model human skull as a gambling mascot recalls a magical practice recorded in Scandinavia, where a real skull was exhumed from a graveyard and from it the spirit of the dead person was summoned to give the necromancer winning lottery numbers.

A model skull has a more general reference to the world of the dead, serving as a lucky charm that may be interpreted as a spirit helper believed to give the gambler an edge. I have in my possession a small ivory skull wearing a top hat that belonged to my grandfather, Charles Pennick (1900–1960), a professional musician who in the 1920s played in an American dance band based in Cleveland, Ohio. He was also an avid gambler, and his lucky mascots were a mixture of American and British practice. In addition to the skull, he possessed a black cat mascot of the cartoon character Felix the Cat, and a cigarette case with an enamel image of a horse, with the name *Rudiobus* beneath it. Rudiobus was an ancient Gaulish horse god (Pennick 2021, 232–223), who was a Celtic god of horses invoked by horse-racing punters. Characteristically, he also smoked Black Cat brand cigarettes.

In America, a black cat crossing one's path is generally considered to be an omen of bad luck, and this applies particularly to anyone who is on their way to a gambling establishment. However, Catherine Yronwode notes that the black cat is also an emblem of

Fig. 9.2. Skull in top hat gambler's charm
used by Charles Pennick, c. 1925.
(Photograph by Nigel Pennick)

luck in adversity, and gamblers in Great Britain and even some in America (for example, see Charles Pennick above) actually use the black cat as a lucky charm. The possession of a black cat's bone is considered to confer both good luck and power upon the owner. It functions in a manner similar to the toad bone used in British toadmanry (Pennick 2019, 67–72).

A Northumbrian practice recorded in 1899 tells that

> he, for instance, who 'maketh haste to be rich' may gain a large sum of money if he can tie up a black cat with ninety-nine knots, and, taking it to the church door, succeed in selling it there to the Devil under the pretence that it is a hare. Such is a Northumbrian belief, but one wonders if even a man from 'canny Newcastle' could so easily deceive the Prince of Darkness. (Tyack 1899, 64)

Any talismans or amulets to be used in gambling magic must be prepared properly and at the appropriate time. As much gambling takes place at night, gambling magic is considered to be part of the magic of darkness—not necessarily in the meaning of "black magic" but in magic intended to operate at night. So we should remember the traditional British practice, recorded by William Bottrell in 1880, that in Cornwall:

> in the spring, people visit a 'Pellar' (cunning man) as soon as there is 'twelve hours' sun,' to have 'their protection renewed,' that is, to be provided with charms; and the wise man's good offices to ward off, for the ensuing year, all evil influences of beings who work in darkness. The reason assigned for observing this particular time is, that 'when the sun is come back the Pellar has more power to good' (do good). (Bottrell 1880, 187)

NUMBERS AND ONE'S FATE

The randomness/determinism interface in the throwing of dice, or on the gambling wheel of fortune when a particular number turns up, is an instance of a moment of irreversible change, like death. Various old soldiers I knew over the years who had fought in the First and Second World Wars as well as the Irish and Spanish Civil Wars, the Korean War and Vietnam War often talked about their number coming up, being doomed to be hit by a bullet with your number on it, and so on. The idea of one having a number may originate from the army's practice of giving each recruit a number by which they were recorded. The orders given to servicemen taken as prisoner of war was to give their name, rank, and number to the enemy but to say nothing else. Every soldier was aware of his name, rank, and number as his identity as a member of the armed forces. When a soldier died on the battlefield, then his comrades reporting it would say "his number's up."

So the idea of a numbered enemy bullet unavoidably hitting its human target with the same number is part of army superstition. The infallible bullet motif comes from shooting magic. It is present in everyday language, for a "magic bullet" means an infallible and rapid solution to a problem, usually used in the negative. A central European magical tradition, that probably dates from the invention of guns, describes how magic bullets can be made, and perhaps the number-bullet connection comes from this. The fabrication of magic bullets that will certainly hit their targets involves calling up the Devil at a crossroads and casting the bullets under his supervision. The bullets are counted as they are made, so they have numbers. Carl Maria von Weber's opera, *Der Freischütz* (1821), that tells of the ritual casting of magic bullets at a crossroads has the proper numerological element in it:

Now the blessing of the bullets!
Bowing to the earth in each of three pauses.
Protect us, you who watch in darkness!
Samiel, Samiel! Give ear!
Stand by me in this night
Till the spell is complete!
Bless for me the herb and lead,
Bless them by seven, nine and three,
That the bullet be obedient!
Samiel, Samiel, to me!

DIVINATION AND
THE DISCOVERY OF
RANDOMNESS

. . . a protest against the rigidity of straight-line thinking

HANS RICHTER

*I*n the twentieth century, just after the Great War had ripped Europe apart with unprecedented levels of death and destruction, Western artists began to explore the random. Contrary to the modernist stance that randomness is analyzable statistically, and thus is under predictable, rational control, artists of the Dada and Surrealist movements explored the unconscious and instinctive rather than the conscious, using the unintentional in preference to the controlled, seeking out the unexpected or unplanned results of chance and randomness. In so doing they instituted a revolt against the modern world, where so much is deemed meaningless. They explored a different consciousness of the random, not as a means of prediction in the traditional way, but rather as a disclosure and manifestation of hidden forces in the world. Hans Richter notes that the "beginning" or "invention" of the use of chance in art in an incident that took place in Hans Arp's studio in the Zeltweg in Zurich in 1920. Arp was dissatisfied with a drawing he was working on, so he tore it up and threw it on the floor of his apartment. Later he noticed the pattern formed by the shreds of paper lying on the floor; it had all the expressive power he had been vainly striving for in his drawing (Richter 1965, 51). Chance had provided expression that the artist had failed to achieve. He stuck the paper down on another sheet in exactly the pattern it had formed when it lay on the floor. Its title is *Nach dem Gesetz des Zufalls* (*According to the Laws of Chance*).

This event led to a discussion on the nature of such happenings, whether the random pattern was the result of the artist's unconscious mind, or whether some external power was operating. Unlike the traditional view of randomness, as manifested in systems of divination, that external, divine powers were operating behind events, the artists left the matter open, exploring without prejudice the nameless no-man's-land that occupies the liminal spaces between the material world, the human psyche and the higher powers of the cosmos. It was speculated that the result might have been from a combination of factors beyond the individual's control, or some "unseen" collaborator directing things. The artist using chance encounters something other than the knowable, a force or power that is present within the artist and the external world, able to liberate the artist from the conventions of art and the banalities of everyday life. Whatever it was, chance had been discovered as a new form of creativity. For the first time, chance was embraced as an essential element of art, a characteristic that distinguished Dada from all previous movements in art.

Recognizing the primacy of chance was a radical attack on dualistic thought, beyond the yes-no and either-or dualities that, paradoxically, are the basis of divination and gambling. Tristan Tzara applied this principle of chance to literature, where he produced poems by tearing many individual words from newspapers, placing them in a bag, and letting them fall from it onto a tabletop. How they fell created a poem. Tzara claimed that this procedure would inevitably reveal something of the mindset and personality of the artist.

Another significant artist of the Dada era was Kurt Schwitters, whose remarkable *Merzbau* installations used found items that had been thrown away or lost in the street—tram tickets, food wrappers, shoelaces, feathers, wire, and so on—random items that laid the foundations for important areas of contemporary art in the twenty-first century. Chance was clearly paramount to what Schwitters used; then again, Schwitters, in the characteristic spirit of Dada, noted in his poem *Lieschen* (the term of endearment translating as "darling"). "There is no such thing as chance. A door may happen to fall shut, but this is not by chance. It is a conscious experience of the door, the door, the door, the door" (Richter 1965, 50).

After World War II, chance was also employed by abstract expressionist artists. For example, André Masson created sand paintings, where he would concentrate for a period, to "switch off" his conscious will, so that his body, his nervous system, and his subconscious would determine where and when the sand would fall onto the canvas. In the 1980s Cage made what he called the *Ryoanji* series, where he produced a contemporary version of Arp's torn paper in another form, by scattering stones at random and drawing around their outlines. In one of these works alone, he drew around 3,375 stones.

Fig. 10.1 Artist Kurt Schwitters's
Hanover Merzbau installation.
(Photo by Wilhelm Redemann, 1933)

CONCLUSION

*D*ivination and gambling have always been close cousins, for they are both instruments of fate that bring irrevocable outcomes. They are two sides of the same coin, so to speak. Whenever we are faced with a momentous decision, it is a moment of crisis, for what we do actually matters, and a wrong decision can mean disaster. Gamblers voluntarily put themselves in this situation every time they wager a large sum upon a racehorse or the roll of the dice. Whereas divination is an engagement that seeks knowledge and the reduction of risk, gambling is an active engagement with the liminal state of randomness, risking all upon it. The gambler puts all of their fortune onto the decisive wheel of Lady Luck alone; the diviner seeks to question all of the powers of existence in the quest for an answer. We are all on the edge, and everything we have can be lost through circumstances without warning. Gamblers actively seek to put themselves into this situation; we who use divination seek to avoid it if at all possible. Divination may give us the edge, but ultimately, win or lose, "wee must dree our wyrd," accepting with good grace whatever "the decree of the Fates" brings us.

Finis

JAMES BALMFORD'S
A SHORT AND PLAINE DIALOGUE

....

*Concerning the Unlawfulnes of Playing
at Cards, or Tables, or Any Other Game
Consisting in Chance, Cambridge, 1593*

The following appendix is a historical record of the conflict between those who enforced religious prohibitions against gaming and those who saw gaming as a harmless, even useful, pastime. In the twenty-first century, only the most extreme theocratic states enforce edicts against play. (The dialogue is between a professor and a preacher and has been edited to standard spelling.)

Professor: Sir, however I am persuaded by that which I read
in the common places of Peter Martyr, paragraph 2,
page 525, b. that dice condemned both by the civil laws and

by the Fathers are therefore unlawful, because they depend upon chance; yet not satisfied with that which he write of table playing, p. 516, and I would crave your opinion concerning playing at tables and cards.

Preacher: Saving the judgment of so excellent a Divine, so far as I can learn out of God's word, cards and tables seem to me no more lawful (though less offensive), than dice. For table playing is no whit the more lawful, because Plato compares the life of man thereunto, than a thief is the more justifiable, because Christ compareth his second coming to burglary in the night (Matt. 24:43, 44). Again, if dice be wholly evil, because they wholly depend upon chance, then tables and cards must need be somewhat evil, because they somewhat depend upon chance. Therefore, consider well this reason, which condemneth the one as well as the other: lots are not to be used in sport; but games consisting in chance, as dice, cards, tables are lots; therefore not to be used in sport.

Professor: For my better instruction, prove that lots are not to be used in sport.

Preacher: Consider with regard these three things: First, that we read not in the Scriptures that lots were used, but only in serious matters, both by the Jews and Gentiles. Secondly, that a lot, in the nature thereof doth as necessarily suppose the special providence and determining presence of God, as an oath in the nature thereof doth suppose the testifying presence of God. Yea, so that, as in an oath, so in a lot, prayer is expressed, or to be understood (1 Sam. 14:41). Thirdly, that the proper end of a lot, as of an oath (Heb. 6:16) is to end a controversy: and, therefore, for your better instruction, examine these reasons. Whatsoever directly, or of itself, or in a special manner, tendeth to the advancing of the name of God, is to be used religiously, and not to be used in sport, as we are not to pray or swear in sport: but the use of lots, directly of itself, and in a special manner, tendeth to the advancing of the name of God, in attributing to his special providence in the whole and immediate disposing of the lot, and expecting the event (Prov. 16:33; Acts 1, 24, 26). Therefore the use of lots is not to be in sport. Again, we are not to tempt the Almighty by a vain desire of manifestation of his power and special providence (P. lxxviii:18, 19; Isa 7:12; Matt. 4:6, 7). But, by using lots in sport, we tempt the Almighty, vainly desiring the manifestation of his special providence in his immediate disposing. Lastly, whatsoever God hath sanctified to a proper end, is not to be perverted to a worse (Matt. 21:12, 13). But God hath sanctified lots to a proper end, namely to end controversies (Num. 26:55; Prov. 18:18), therefore man is not to pervert them to a worse, namely to play, and, by playing to get away another man's money, which, without controversy, is his own. For the common saying is, *Sine lucro friget lusus,* no gaining, cold gaming.

Professor: God hath sanctified Psalms to the praise of his name, and bread and wine to represent the body and blood of our crucified Savior, which be holy ends; and the children of God may sing Psalms to make themselves merry in the Lord, and feed upon bread and wine, not only from necessity, but to cheer themselves; why, then, may not God's children recreate themselves by lottery, notwithstanding God hath sanctified the same to end a controversy?

Preacher: Because we find not in the Scriptures any dispensation for recreation by lottery, as we do for godly mirth by singing

(James 13), and for religious and sober cheering ourselves by eating and drinking (Deut. 8:9, 10). And, therefore (it being with all considered that the ends you speak of, be not proper, though holy), it followeth, that God who only disposeth the lot touching the event, and is, therefore, a principal actor, is not to be set on work by lottery in any case, but when he dispenseth with us, or gives us leave so to do. But dispensation for recreation by lottery cannot be shown.

Professor: Lots may be used for profit in a matter of right (Num. 26:55), why not, for pleasure?

Preacher: Then oaths may be used for pleasure, for they may for profit, in a matter of truth (Exod. 22:8, 11). But, indeed, lots (as oaths), are not to be used for profit or pleasure, but only to end a controversy.

Professor: The wit is exercised by tables and cards, therefore they be no lots.

Preacher: Yet lottery is used by casting dice, and by shuffling and cutting, before the wit is exercised. But how does this follow? Because cards and tables be not naked lots, consisting only in chance (as dice) they are, therefore, no lots at all. Although (being used without cogging, or packing) they consist principally in chance, from whence they are to receive denomination. In which respect, a lot is called in Latin, Sors, that is, chance or hazard. And Lyra upon Prov. 16 saith, To use lots, is, by a variable event of some sensible thing, to determine some doubtful or uncertain matter, as to draw cuts, or to cast dice. But, whether you will call cards and tables, lots, or not, you play with chance, or use lottery. Then, consider whether exercise of wit does sanctify playing with lottery, or playing with lottery make such exercising of wit a sin (Hag. 2:13, 14). For as calling God to witness by vain swearing, is a sin (2 Cor. 1:13), so making God an umpire, by playing with lottery, must needs be a sin; yea, such a sin as maketh the offender (in some respects) more blame worthy. For there be more occasions of swearing than of lottery. Secondly, vain oaths most commonly slip out unawares, whereas lots cannot be used but with deliberation. Thirdly, swearing is to satisfy other, whereas this kind of lottery is altogether to fulfill our own lusts. Therefore, take heed, that you be not guilty of perverting the ordinance of the Lord, of taking the name of God in vain, and of tempting the Almighty, by a gamesome putting off things to hazard, and making play of lottery, except you think that God hath no government in vain actions, or hath dispensed with such lewd games.

Professor: In shooting, there is a chance, by a sudden blast, yet shooting is no lottery.

Preacher: It is true; for chance commeth by accident, and not of the nature of the game, to be used.

Professor: Lots are secret, and the whole disposing of them is of God (Prov. 16:33); but it is otherwise in tables and cards.

Preacher: Lots are cast into the lap by man, and that openly, lest conveyance should be suspected; but the disposing of the chance is secret, that it may be chance indeed, and wholly of God, who directeth all things (Prov. 16:13, 9, 33). So in tables, man by fair casting dice truly made, and in cards, by shuffling and cutting, doth openly dispose the dice and cards so, as whereby a variable event may follow; but it is only and immediately of God that the dice be so cast, and the cards so shuffled and cut, as that this or that game followeth, except there be cogging and packing. So that, in fair play, man's wit is not exercised in disposing the chance, but in making the best of it, being past.

Professor: The end of our play is recreation, and not to make God an umpire; but recreation (no doubt) is lawful.

Preacher: It may be the soldiers had no such end when they cast lots for Christ his coat (Matt. 27:25), but this should be your end when you use lottery, as the end of an oath should be, to call God to witness. Therefore, as swearing, so lottery, without due respect, is sin. Again, howsoever recreation be your pretended end, yet, remember that we must not doe evil that good may come of it (Rom. 3:8). And that therefore we are to recreate ourselves by lawful recreations. Then see how cards and tables be lawful.

Professor: If they be not abused by swearing or brawling, playing for too long a time, or too much money.

Preacher: Though I am persuaded that it is not lawful to play for any money, considering that thanks cannot be given in faith for that which is so gotten (Deut. 23:18, Isa. Ixi:8) Gamesters work not with their hands the thing that is good, to be free from stealing (Eph. 4:28), and the loser hath not answerable benefit for his money so lost (Gen. 24:15) contrary to that equity, which Aristotle, by the light of nature hath taught long since; yet I grant, if cards and tables, so used as you speak, be less sinful, but how they be lawful I see not yet.

Professor: Good men, and well learned, use them.

Preacher: We must live by precept, not by examples, except they be undoubtedly good. Therefore, examine whether they be good and well learned in doing so, or no. For every man may err (Rom. 3:4).

Professor: It is not good to be too just, or too wise (Eccl. 7:18).

Preacher: It is not good to be too wise, or too foolish, in despising the word of God (Prov. 1: 22) and not regarding the weakness of other (Rom. 14:21). Let us therefore beware that we love not pleasure more than godliness (2 Tim. 3:4).

THE OFFICIALS OF GAMBLING HOUSES, LONDON, 1731

The first number of *Gentleman's Magazine* in 1731 published a list of functionaries who operated the most notorious gaming houses in London:

1. A Commissioner, always a Proprietor, who looks in of a Night, and the Week's Accompt [account] is audited by him, and two others of the Proprietors.
2. A Director; who superintends the Room.
3. An Operator; who deals the Cards at a cheating Game, called Faro.
4. Two Crowpees [croupiers] who watch the Cards, and gather the Money for the Bank.
5. Two Puffs, who have Money given them to decoy others to play.

6. A Clerk, who is a Check upon the Puffs, to see that they sink none of the Money that is given them to play with.

7. A Squib, is a Puff of a lower Rank, who serves at half Salary, while he is learning to deal.

8. A Flasher, to swear how often the Bank has been stript.

9. A Dunner, who goes about to recover Money lost at Play.

10. A Waiter, to fill out Wine, snuff Candles, and attend in the Gaming Room.

11. An Attorney, a Newgate Solicitor.

12. A Captain who is to fight a Gentleman that is peevish at losing his money.

13. An Usher, who lights Gentlemen up and down Stairs, and gives the Word to the Porter.

14. A Porter, who is, generally, a Soldier of the Foot Guards.

15. An Orderly Man, who walks up and down the outside of the Door, to give Notice to the Porter, and alarm the House, at the Approach of the Constables.

16. A Runner, who is to get Intelligence of the Justices meeting.

17. Linkboys, Coachmen, Chairmen, Drawers, or others, who bring the first Intelligence of the Justices Meetings, or, of the Constables being out, at Half a Guinea Reward.

18. Common Bail Affidavit Men, Ruffians, Bravoes, Assassins, *cum multis aliis* (Ashton 1898, 56–57).

BIBLIOGRAPHY

Abimbola, Wande. 1977. *Ifa Divination Poetry*. New York: Nok Publishers.

Adams, William H. Davenport. 1895. *Witch, Warlock and Magician: Historical Sketches of Magic and Witchcraft in England and Scotland*. London: Chatto and Windus.

Adler, Alfred, and Andras Zempléni. 1972. *Le bâton de l'aveugle: Divination, maladie et pouvoir chez les Moundang du Tchad*. Paris: Hermann.

Ambelain, Robert. 1940. *La Géomancie Magique*. Paris: Niclaus.

Ashton, John. 1893. *A History of English Lotteries: Now for the First Time Written*. London: Leadenhall Press.

———. 1898. *The History of Gambling in England*. London: Duckworth.

Bales, E. G. 1939. "Folklore from West Norfolk." *Folklore* 50, no. 1 (March 1939): 66–75.

Balmford, James. 1593. *A Short and Plaine Dialogue Concerning the Unlawfulnes of Playing at Cards, or Tables, or Any Other Game Consisting in Chance*. Cambridge.

Bascom, William. 1969. *Ifa Divination: Communication between Gods and Men in West Africa*. Bloomington: Indiana University Press.

———. 1980. *Sixteen Cowries. Yoruba Divination from Africa to the New World*. Bloomington: Indiana University Press.

Bean, J. P. 1981. *The Sheffield Gang Wars*. Sheffield, UK: D & D Publications.

Bennett, Deborah J. 1998. *Randomness,* Cambridge: Harvard University Press.

Besant, Annie, and C. W. Leadbeater. 1901. *Thought-Forms*. London: Theosophical Publishing House.

Bottrell, William. 1880. *Stories and Folk-Lore of West Cornwall*. Penzance, UK: F. Rodda.

Bouché-Leclercq, A. 1975. *Histoire de la divination dans l'antiquité*. 2 vols. New York: Arno Press.

Breton, André. 1974. *Manifestos of Surrealism*. Translated by Richard Seaver, and Helen R. Lane. Ann Arbor: University of Michigan Press.

Cage, John (interviewed by Birger Ollrogge). 1997. *October* 82 (Autumn).

Campbell, Alec C. 1968. "Some Notes on Ngwaketse Divination." *Botswana Notes and Records* 1: 9–13.

Campbell, Helen, Thomas Knox, and Thomas Byrnes. 1892. *Darkness and Daylight; Or, Lights and Shadows of New York Life*. New York: A. D. Worthington & Co.

Canney, Maurice A. 1926. "The Use of Sand in Magic and Religion." *Man* (January): 13.

Carpenter, Edward. 1912. *The Art of Creation. Essays on the Self and Its Powers*. London: George Allan.

Carr-Gomm, Philip, and Richard Heygate. 2010. *The Book of English Magic*. London: John Murray.

Cassirer, Ernst. 1945. *Language and Myth*. New York: Dover.

Chaitin, Gregory. 2001. *Exploring Randomness*. London: Springer-Verlag.

Champeaux, Jacqueline. 1982. *Fortuna: Recherches sur le culte de la Fortuna à Rome et dans le monde romaine des origines à la mort de César*. Rome: École Française de Rome.

———. 1987. *Fortuna: Les Transformations de Fortuna sous le République*. Rome: École Française de Rome.

Chapman, Rod. 2007. *Seven: An Idiosyncratic Look at the Number Seven*, North Elmham, UK: Seven Star Publishing.

de Chirico, Giorgio. 1929. *Hebdemeros*. Paris: Carrefour.

Chomsky, Noam. 1977. "Objectivity and Liberal Scholarship." *The Cienfuegos Press Anarchist Review* 1, no. 3: 38–58.

Christian, Paul. 1972. *The History and Practice of Magic.* Translated by James Kirkup and Julian Shaw. Edited by Ross Nichols. Secaucus, N.J.: The Citadel Press.

Cotton, Charles. 1674. *The Compleat Gamester.* London: A.M.

Cronin, Anthony. 1989. *No Laughing Matter: The Life and Times of Flann O'Brien.* London: Grafton Books.

Curnow, Trevor. 2004. *Oracles of the Ancient World.* London: Duckworth.

Dalí, Salvador. 1935. *La conquète de l'irrationel.* Paris: Surréalistes.

Darnton, Robert. 1984. "The Great Cat Massacre, 1730." *History Today* 34 (August): 7–15.

Deacon, Richard. 1977. *Napoleon's Book of Fate: Its Origins and Uses.* Secaucus, N.J.: Citadel Press.

Decker, Ronald, and Michael Dummett. 2002. *A History of the Occult Tarot 1870–1970.* London: Duckworth.

Disney, John. 1729. *A View of Ancient Laws against Immorality and Profaneness.* Cambridge.

Dornan, S. S. 1923. "Divination and Divining Bones." *South African Journal of Science,* 20: 504–11.

Eiselen, W. M. 1932. "The Art of Divination as Practised by the Bamasemola." *Bantu Studies* 6: 1–29, 251–63.

Eliade, Mircea. 1959. *The Sacred and the Profane.* New York: Harcourt, Brace, Jovanovitch.

Emmison, F. G. 1970. *Elizabethan Life: Disorder.* Chelmsford, UK: Essex Record Office.

Evans-Wentz, W. Y. 1911. *The Fairy Faith in Celtic Countries.* London: Oxford University Press.

Fahd, Toufic. 1966. *La divination arabe: Etudes religieuses sociologiques et folkloriques sur le milieu natif de l'Islam.* Leiden, NL: Brill.

Ferrand, Gabriel. 1905. "Un chapitre d'astrologie arabo-malgache." *Journal asiatique* (September–October): 193–273.

Finn, Timothy. 1975. *Pub Games of England.* Cambridge: Oleander Press.

Fiske, Daniel Willard. 1905. *Chess in Iceland and in Icelandic Literature with Historical Notes on Other Table-Games.* Florence: The Florentine Typographical Society.

Flowers, Stephen. 1989. *The Galdrabók: An Icelandic Grimoire.* York Beach, Maine: Samuel Weiser.

Fortune, Dion. 1933. "Ceremonial Magic Unveiled." *The Occult Review* 57 (January): 13–24.

Garbutt, H. W. 1909. "Native Witchcraft and Superstition in South Africa." *Proceedings of the Rhodesia Scientific Association* 9: 40–80.

Gelfand, Michael. 1964. *Witch Doctor: Traditional Medicine Man of Rhodesia,* London: Harvill Press.

Gerard of Cremona. 1978. *Fourth Book of Occult Philosophy* (1655). London: Askin Publishers.

Gleason, Judith. 1973. *A Recitation of Ifa: Oracle of the Yoruba.* New York: Grossman Publishers.

Golding, John. 2000. *Paths to the Absolute. Mondrian, Malevitch, Kandinsky, Pollock, Newman, Rothko and Still.* London: Thames & Hudson.

Götze, Alfred. 1918. Foreword to and notes of *Das Straßburger Würfelbuch von 1529.* Strasbourg: Karl J. Trübner.

Groves, Derham. 1991. *Feng-Shui and Western Building Ceremonies.* Singapore: Graham Brash.

Hand, Wayland. 1980. *Magical Medicine: The Folkloric Component of Medicine in the Folk Belief, Custom and Rituals of the Peoples of Europe and America.* Berkeley: University of California Press.

Hasenfratz, Hans-Peter. 2011. *Barbarian Rites. The Spiritual World of the Vikings and the Germanic Tribes.* Translated by Michael Moynihan. Rochester, Vt.: Inner Traditions.

Hébert, J. C. 1961. "Analyse structural des géomancies comoriennes, malgaches et africaines." *Journal de la Societé des Africainistes* 31, no. 2: 115–208.

Hewett, Sarah. 1900. *Nummits and Crummits: Devonshire Customs.* London: Thomas Burleigh.

Hewison, Robert. 1987. *The Heritage Industry.* London: Methuen.

Hiller, Susan. 1995. *After the Freud Museum.* London: Book Works.

Howe, Ellic. 1964. *Raphael, or the Royal Merlin.* London: Arborfield.

Hunt, N. 1950. "Some Notes on Witchdoctor's Bones." *Native Affairs Department Annual* 27: 40–46.

———. 1954. "Some Notes on Witchdoctor's Bones." *Native Affairs Department Annual* 31: 16–23.

———. 1962. "More Notes on Witchdoctor's Bones." *Native Affairs Department Annual* 39: 14–16.

Hurston, Zora N. 1931. "Hoodoo in America." *The Journal of American Folklore* 44: 317–417.

Hyatt, Harry Middleton. 1970–1978. *Hoodoo, Conjuration, Witchcraft, Rootwork.* 5 vols. Memoirs of the Alma Egan Hyatt Foundation.

Jacobsen-Widding, Anita. 1979. *Red-White-Black as a Mode of Thought.* Uppsala Studies in Cultural Anthropology I. Stockholm: Almqvist and Wiksell.

de Jager, E. J., and O. M. Seboni. 1964. "Bone Divination among the Kwena of Molepolole District, Bechuanaland Protectorate." *Afrika und Übersee* 48: 2–16.

Jaulin, R. 1966. *La géomancie: analyse formelle.* Volume 4 of *Cahiers de l'homme: ethnologie, géographie, linguistique,* Paris: Mouton.

Jordán, Manuel. 1994. "Heavy Stuff and Heavy Staffs from the Chokwe and Related Peoples of Angola, Zaire, and Zambia." In *Staffs of Life.* Edited by A. F. Roberts. Iowa City: University of Iowa Museum of Art.

Junod, H. A. 1925. "La divination au moyen de tablettes d'ivoire chez les Pedis." *Bulletin de la Société de Neuchatel de Géographie* (Doc Rer Ch website) 34: 38–56.

Kallenberg, Olav. 1986. *Random Measures.* New York: Academic Press.

Knuth, Donald E. 1997. *The Art of Computer Programming. Vol. 2: Seminumerical Algorithms.* Reading, UK: Addison-Wesley.

Kretschmer, Fritz. n.d. *Bilddokumente römischer Technik.* Wiesbaden: Panorama Verlag.

Lachatañere, Romulu. 1942. *Manual de Santeria.* Havana: Editorial Caribe.

Laydevant, F. 1933. "The Praises of the Divining Bones among the Basutho." *Bantu Studies* 7: 341–73.

Levitas, Ruth. 1991. *The Concept of Utopia.* Syracuse: Syracuse University Press.

Lucas, Theophilus. 1714. *Memoirs of the Lives, Intrigues, and Comical Adventures of the Most Famous Gamesters and Celebrated Sharpers in the Reigns of Charles II, James II, William III, and Queen Anne.* London.

Lyndoe, Edward. 1935. *Everybody's Book of Fate and Fortune*. London: Odhams.

Maddern, Philippa. 2004. "Order and Disorder." In *Medieval Norwich*. Edited by Carole Rawcliffe and Richard Wilson. London: Hambledon and London, 189–212.

Malcolm, James Peller. 1810. *Anecdotes of the Manners and Customs of London during the 18th Century*. London: Longman, Hurst, Rees and Oram.

Malraux, André. 1954. *The Voices of Silence*. London: Secker & Warburg.

Matless, David. 1993. "Appropriate Geography: Patrick Abercrombie and the Energy of the World." *Journal of Design History* 6: 168.

Maupoil, Bernard. 1943. "La Géomancie à l'ancienne Côte des Esclaves." *Travaux et Mémoires de l'Institut d'Ethnologie* 42, no. 27.

———. 1943. "Contribution à l'origine musulmane de la géomancie dans le Bas-Dahomey." *Journal de la Société des Africanistes* 13.

McClelland, Gordon. 1980. *Rick Griffin*. Limpsfield, UK: Paper Tiger.

Miller, George A. 1956. "The Magical Number Seven, Plus or Minus Two: Some Limits on Our Capacity for Processing Information." *The Psychological Review* 62, no. 3.

Mlodinow, Leonard. 2008. *The Drunkard's Walk: How Randomness Rules Our Lives*. New York: Pantheon Books.

Monteil, C. 1931. "La divination chez les Noirs de l'O.A.F. [Afrique Occidentale Française]." *Bulletin du Comité d'études historiques et scientifiques de l'Afrique Occidentale Française* 14, no. 1/2: 72–136.

Nataf, André. 1994. *Dictionary of the Occult*. Translated by John Davidson. Ware, UK: Wordsworth Editions.

Needham, Rodney. 1981. *Circumstantial Deliveries*. Berkeley: University of California Press.

O'Brien, Flann. 1993. "The Myles na gCopaleen Catechism of Cliché." In *The Best of Myles: A Selection from "Cruiskeen Lawn."* London: Flamingo, 201–27.

Otto, Rudolf. 1973. *The Idea of the Holy*. New York: Oxford University Press.

Peacock, Mabel Geraldine W. 1897. "Omens Of Death." *Folk-Lore* 8: 377–78.

Peek, Philip M. ed. 1991. *African Divination Systems: Ways of Knowing*. Bloomington: Indiana University Press.

Pemberton, John, III. ed. 2000. *Insight and Artistry in African Divination.* Washington: Smithsonian Institution Press.

Pennick, Nigel.

————. 1976. *Madagascar Divination.* Bar Hill, UK: Fenris-Wolf.

————. 1985. *Hugin and Munin Rune Cards.* Bar Hill, UK:Fenris-Wolf.

————. 1986. *Brett und Stein und Zauber.* Horgenzell: Neue Erde.

————. 1986. *Skulls, Cats and Witch Bottles.* Bar Hill, UK: Nigel Pennick Editions.

————. 1990. *Das Runen Orakel.* München: Knaur Esoterik.

————. 1994. *Geomancy.* Numbered limited edition of twelve card decks. Bar Hill, UK: Nideck.

————. 1995. *The Oracle of Geomancy: The Divinatory Arts of Raml, Geomantia, Sikidy and I Ching.* Chieveley, UK: Capall Bann.

————. 2003. *Ursprünge der Weissagung: Von Orakeln, Heligen Zahlen und Magischen Quadraten.* Düsseldorf: Patmos Verlag.

————. 2006. *Folk-Lore of East Anglia and Adjoining Counties.* Bar Hill, UK: Spiritual Arts & Crafts Publishing.

————. 2011. *The Toadman.* Hinckley, UK: The Society of Esoteric Endeavour.

————. 2012. "The Overlooked Histories of Snakes' Eyes and the Ace of Spades." In *The Starry Rubric Set.* Edited by Gareth Bell-Jones and An Endless Supply. Bourn, UK: Wysing Arts Centre.

————. 2019. *Witchcraft and Secret Societies of Rural England: The Magic of Toadmen, Plough Witches. Mummers and Bonesmen.* Rochester, Vt.: Destiny Books. First published as *In Field and Fen* by Lear Books, 2011.

————. 2021. *The Ancestral Power of Amulets, Talismans, and Mascots. Folk Magic in Witchcraft and Religion.* Rochester Vt.: Destiny Books.

Pennick, Nigel, and Nigel Jackson. 1992. *The Celtic Oracle.* Aquarian Press: London.

Peyre de Mandiargues, André. 1948. *Les Incongruités monumentales.* Paris: Laffont.

Pleij, Herman. 2001. *Dreaming of Cockaigne. Medieval Fantasies of the Perfect Life.* Translated by Diane Webb. New York: Columbia University Press.

Rayson, George. 1865. "East Anglian Folk-Lore, No. 2 'Omens.'" *The East Anglian, or, Notes and Queries on Subjects Connected with the Counties of Suffolk, Cambridgeshire, Essex and Norfolk* 1: 185–6.

Regier, Kathleen J., comp. 1987. *The Spiritual Image in Modern Art*. Wheaton: Theosophical Publishing House.

Reynolds, Barrie. 1963. *Magic, Divination and Witchcraft among the Barotse of Northern Rhodesia*. Berkeley: University of California Press.

Richter, Hans. 1965. *Dada. Art and Anti-Art*. London: Thames & Hudson.

Roberts, Noel. 1915. "A Few Notes on *To Kolo:* A System of Divination Practiced by the Superior Natives of Malaboch's Tribe in Northern Transvaal." *South African Journal of Science* 11: 367–70.

Roper, Charles. 1883. "On Witchcraft Superstition in Norfolk." *Harper's New Monthly Magazine* 87, no. 521 (October): 792–97.

Roud, Steve. 2003. *The Penguin Guide to the Superstitions of Britain and Ireland*. London: Penguin Books.

Rouget, Gilbert. 1985. *Music and Trance*. Chicago: University of Chicago Press.

Samuel, Raphael, and Paul Thompson (eds.). 1990. *The Myths We Live By*. London: Routledge.

Sapir, David. 1977. "The Anatomy of Metaphor." In *The Social Use of Metaphor: Essays on the Anthropology of Rhetoric*. Edited by J. D. Sapir and C. Crocker. Philadelphia: University of Pennsylvania Press.

Scarne, John. 1980. *Scarne on Dice*. Hollywood: Melvin Powers Wilshire Book Company.

Scott, Nathan. 1966. *The Broken Center: Studies in the Theological Horizon of Modern Literature*. New Haven: Yale University Press.

Seligmann, Kurt. 1942. "Magic Circles." *View* 1 (February–March): 3.

Senn, Stephen. 2003. *Dicing with Death: Chance, Risk and Health*. Cambridge: Cambridge University Press.

von Sicard, H. 1959. "The Hakata Names." *Native Affairs Department Annual* 36: 26–29.

Singer, William. 1881. *An Exposition of the Miller and Horseman's Word, or the True System of Raising the Devil*. Aberdeen: James Daniel.

Skinner, Stephen. 1977. *The Oracle of Geomancy*, New York: Warner Destiny.

———. 1980. *Terrestrial Astrology. Divination by Geomancy*. London: Routledge & Kegan Paul.

Sperber, Dan. 1975. *Rethinking Symbolism*. Cambridge: Cambridge University Press.

Souter, Helen Greig. n.d. *Signs and Superstitions*.

The Symbol. 1983. Volume 1, Cambridge, UK: The Society for Symbolic Studies, 12.

Trautmann, René. 1940. *La divination à la Côte des Esclaves et à la Madagascar: Le Vôdoû Fa—Le Sikidy*. Mémoires de l'Institut Français d'Afrique Noire, no. 1. Paris: Larose.

Trigg, Elwood B. 1973. *Gypsy Demons and Divinities: The Magical and Supernatural Practices of the Gypsies*. London: Sheldon Press.

Turner, Victor. 1969. *The Ritual Process: Structure and Anti-Structure*. Chicago: University of Chicago Press.

Tyack, George S. 1899. *Lore and Legend of the English Church*. London: William Andrews.

Tzara, Tristan. 1930. *L'Homme approximatif*. Paris: Fourcade.

Villiers, Elizabeth. 1923. *The Mascot Book*. London: T. Werner Laurie.

von Weber, Carl Maria. 1821. *Der Freischütz*. Opera.

Werbner, Richard P. 1989. *Ritual Passage, Sacred Journey*. Manchester: Manchester University Press.

Wither, George. 1635. *A Collection of Emblemes, Ancient and Moderne*. London.

Wittkower, Rudolf. 1963. *Born Under Saturn*. New York: W. W. Norton & Co..

Wright, A. R., and Edward Lovett. 1908. "Specimens of Modern Mascots and Ancient Amulets of the British Isles." *Folk-Lore* 19, no. 3 (September): 283–303.

W. W. N. 1899. "Negro Superstitions of European Origin." *The Journal of American Folk-Lore* 12, no. 47 (October–December): 294–95.

INDEX